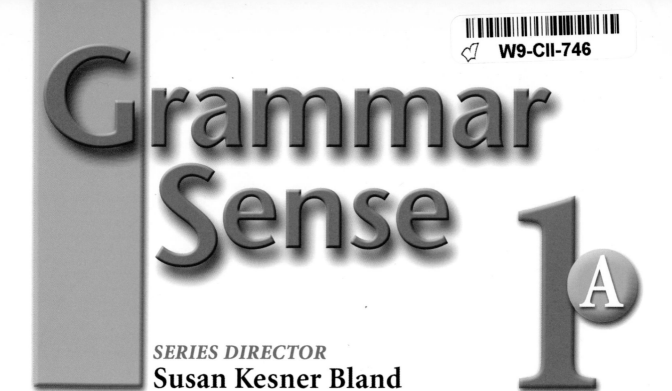

Grammar Sense 1A

SERIES DIRECTOR
Susan Kesner Bland

Cheryl Pavlik

OXFORD

UNIVERSITY PRESS

OXFORD
UNIVERSITY PRESS

198 Madison Avenue
New York, NY 10016 USA

Great Clarendon Street
Oxford OX2 6DP England

Oxford New York

Auckland Bangkok Buenos Aires Cape Town Chennai
Dar es Salaam Delhi Hong Kong Istanbul Karachi Kolkata
Kuala Lumpur Madrid Melbourne Mexico City Mumbai
Nairobi São Paulo Shanghai Taipei Tokyo Toronto

OXFORD is a trademark of Oxford University Press.

Copyright © 2004 Oxford University Press

ISBN 0-19-436567-0 Student Book

ISBN 0-19-439714-9 Student Book with Grammar Wizard (pack)

The Library of Congress has catalogued the full edition as:

Pavlik, Cheryl, 1949-
　　Grammar Sense 1 / series director, Susan Kesner Bland;
Cheryl Pavlik.
　　　p. cm.
　　Includes index.
　　ISBN 0-19-436565-4
　　1. English language—Textbooks for foreign speakers. 2. English
language—Grammar—Problems, exercises, etc. I. Title: Grammar
Sense one. II. Bland, Susan Kesner. III. Title.

PE1128.P374 2004
428.2'4—dc21   2003054875

Editorial Manager: Janet Aitchison
Senior Editor: Stephanie Karras
Editor: Pietro Alongi
Associate Editors: Katya MacDonald, Ashli Totty
Art Director: Lynn Luchetti
Design Manager: Mary Chandler
Designer (cover): Lee Anne Dollison
Senior Art Editor: Jodi Waxman
Art Editor: Judi DeSouter
Production Manager: Shanta Persaud
Production Controller: Eve Wong

Book Design: Bill Smith Studio
Composition: Compset, Inc.
Indexer: Leonard Neufeld

Printing (last digit): 10 9 8 7 6 5 4 3 2 1

Printed in Hong Kong.

Acknowledgments

Cover image: © Kevin Schafer / Peter Arnold, Inc.

Illustrations by:
Barbara Bastian, Lyndall Culbertson, Paul Hampson,
Mike Hortens, Randy Jones, Jon Keegan, Raymond Lee,
Scott MacNeill, Laura Hartman Maestro, Karen Minot,
Tom Newsom, Roger Penwill, Alan Reingold, Don Stewart,
Bill Thomson

*The publisher would like to thank the following for
their permission to reproduce photographs:*
Action-Plus; Alamy images; Bananastock; Bettman/Corbis;
Stefano Bianchetti/Corbis; Bruce Burhardt / Corbis; Jacques M.
Chenet / Corbis; Chicago Historical Society; Comstock; Philip
James Corwin / Corbis; Corbis; Courtesy of the Bostonian Society
/ Old State House; CUMULUS; Araldo de Luca / Corbis; Lee
Anne Dollison / OUP; Getty; Hulton-Deutsch Collection / Corbis;
ImageState; Index Stock Imagery; Karen Minot; PhotoDisc;
PhotoDisc Green; Pictures Coulour Library; Anthony
Redpath/Corbis; Robert Harding World Imagery; Rochester
Democrat & Chronicle / Corbis Sygma; Royalty-Free / Corbis;
Ariel Skelley / Corbis; StockPhotoAsia; SuperStock; Syracuse
Newspapers / The Image Works; Brian Sytnyk / Masterfile; Liba
Taylor / Corbis; Tim Thompson / Corbis; Jodi Waxman/OUP;
Michael S. Yamashita / Corbis

Acknowledgements

It takes a village to write a grammar series. I am humbled by the expertise of all those who have contributed in so many ways.

I am grateful to Cheryl Pavlik for her intellectual curiosity, creativity, wit, and for her friendship. A special thanks goes to Stephanie Karras for putting all of the pieces together with such commitment and superb organizational and problem-solving skills, mixed with just the right amount of levity. I owe a special debt of gratitude to Janet Aitchison for her continued support and encouragement from the very beginning, and for her help with the big issues as well as the small details.

It has been a pleasure working closely with Diane Flanel Piniaris, Pietro Alongi, Andrew Gitzy, James Morgan, Nan Clarke, Randee Falk, and Marietta Urban. Their comments, questions, grammar insights, and creative solutions have been invaluable. Many thanks also go to the talented editorial, production, and design staff at Oxford University Press; to Susan Lanzano for her role in getting this project started; and to Susan Mraz for her help in the early stages.

Finally, I owe everything to my family, Bob, Jenny, and Scott, for always being there for me, as well as for their amusing views about everything, especially grammar.

Susan Kesner Bland,
Series Director

The Series Director and Publisher would like to acknowledge the following individuals for their invaluable input during the development of this series:

Harriet Allison, Atlanta College of Art, GA; **Alex Baez,** Southwest Texas State University, TX; **Nathalie Bailey,** Lehman College, CUNY, NY; **Jamie Beaton,** Boston University, MA; **Michael Berman,** Montgomery College, MD; **Angela Blackwell,** San Francisco State University, CA; **Vera Bradford,** IBEU, Rio de Janerio, Brazil; **Glenda Bro,** Mount San Antonio Community College, CA; **Jennifer Burton,** University of California, San Francisco, CA; **Magali Duignan,** Augusta State University, GA; **Anne Ediger,** Hunter College, CUNY, NY; **Joyce Grabowski,** Flushing High School, NY; **Virginia Heringer,** Pasadena City College, CA; **Rocia Hernandez,** Mexico City, Mexico; **Nancy Herzfeld-Pipkin,** University of California, San Diego, CA; **Michelle Johnstone,** Mexico City, Mexico; **Kate de Jong,** University of California, San Diego, CA; **Pamela Kennedy,** Holyoke Community College, MA; **Jean McConochie,** Pace University, NY; **Karen McRobie,** Golden Gate University, CA; **Elizabeth Neblett,** Union County College, NJ; **Dian Perkins,** Wheeling High School, IL; **Fausto Rocha de Marcos Rebelo,** Recife, Brazil; **Mildred Rugger,** Southwest Texas State University, TX; **Dawn Schmidt,** California State University, San Marcos, CA; **Katharine Sherak,** San Francisco State University, CA; **Lois Spitzer,** University of Nebraska-Lincoln, NE; **Laura Stering,** University of California, San Francisco, CA; **Annie Stumpfhauser,** Morelios, Mexico; **Anthea Tillyer,** Hunter College, CUNY, NY; **Julie Un,** Massasoit Community College, MA; **Susan Walker,** SUNY New Paltz, NY; **Cheryl Wecksler,** California State University, San Marcos, CA; **Teresa Wise,** Georgia State University, GA.

Contents

PART 3: Adjectives and Pronouns

PART 4: The Present

Introduction

Grammar Sense: A Discourse-Based Approach

Grammar Sense is a comprehensive three-level grammar series based on the authentic use of English grammar in discourse. The grammar is systematically organized, explained, and practiced in a communicative, learner-centered environment, making it easily teachable and learnable.

Many people ask, why learn grammar? The answer is simple: meaningful communication depends on our ability to connect form and meaning appropriately. In order to do so, we must consider such factors as intention, attitude, and social relationships, in addition to the contexts of time and place. All of these factors make up a discourse setting. For example, we use the present continuous not only to describe an activity in progress *(He's working.)*, but also to complain *(He's always working.)*, to describe a planned event in the future *(He's working tomorrow.)*, and to describe temporary or unusual behavior *(He's being lazy at work.)*. It is only through examination of the discourse setting that the different meanings and uses of the present continuous can be distinguished from one another. A discourse-based approach provides students with the tools for making sense of the grammar of natural language by systematically explaining *who, what, where, when, why,* and *how* for each grammatical form.

Systematically Organized Syllabus

Learning grammar is a developmental process that occurs gradually. In *Grammar Sense* the careful sequencing, systematic repetition, recycling, review, and expansion promote grammatical awareness and fluency.

Level 1 (basic level) focuses on building an elementary understanding of form, meaning, and use as students develop basic oral language skills in short conversations and discussions. Level 1 also targets the grammar skills involved in writing short paragraphs, using basic cohesive devices such as conjunctions and pronouns.

At **Level 2 (intermediate level)** the focus turns to expanding the basic understanding of form, meaning, and use in longer and more varied discourse settings, and with more complex grammatical structures and academic themes. Level 2 emphasizes grammar skills beyond the sentence level, as students begin to initiate and sustain conversations and discussions, and progress toward longer types of writing.

Finally, at **Level 3 (high intermediate to advanced level)** the focus moves to spoken and written grammar in academic discourse settings, often in contexts that are conceptually more challenging and abstract. Level 3 emphasizes consistent and appropriate language use, especially of those aspects of grammar needed in extended conversations and discussions, and in longer academic and personal writing.

Introduction of Form Before Meaning and Use

Form is introduced and practiced in a separate section before meaning and use. This ensures that students understand what the form looks like and sounds like at the sentence level, before engaging in more challenging and open-ended activities that concentrate on meaning and use.

Focus on Natural Language Use

Grammar Sense uses authentic reading texts and examples that are based on or quoted verbatim from actual English-language sources to provide a true picture of natural language use. To avoid unnatural language, the themes of the introductory reading texts are only subtly touched upon throughout a chapter. The focus thus remains on typical examples of the most common meanings and uses.

Exposure to authentic language helps students bridge the gap between the classroom and the outside world by encouraging awareness of the "grammar" all around them in daily life: in magazines, newspapers, package instructions, television shows, signs, and so on. Becoming language-aware is an important step in the language-learning process: Students generalize from the examples they find and apply their understanding to their independent language use in daily living, at work, or as they further their education.

Special Sections to Extend Grammatical Knowledge

Understanding grammar as a system entails understanding how different parts of the language support and interact with the target structure. *Grammar Sense* features special sections at strategic points throughout the text to highlight relevant lexical and discourse issues.

- **Beyond the Sentence** sections focus on the structure as it is used in extended discourse to help improve students' writing skills. These sections highlight such issues as how grammatical forms are used to avoid redundancy, and how to change or maintain focus.

- **Informally Speaking** sections highlight the differences between written and spoken language. This understanding is crucial for achieving second language fluency. Reduced forms, omissions, and pronunciation changes are explained in order to improve aural comprehension.

- **Pronunciation Notes** show students how to pronounce selected forms of the target language, such as the regular simple past ending -*ed*.

- **Vocabulary Notes** provide succinct presentations of words and phrases that are commonly used with the target structure, such as time expressions associated with the simple present and simple past.

Student-Centered Presentation and Practice

Student-centered presentation and practice allow learners at all levels to discover the grammar in pairs, groups, and individually, in both the Form and in the Meaning and Use sections of each chapter. Numerous inductive activities encourage students to use their problem-solving abilities to gain the skills, experience, and confidence to use English outside of class and to continue learning on their own.

Flexibility to Suit Any Classroom Situation

Grammar Sense offers teachers great flexibility with hundreds of intellectually engaging exercises to choose from. Teachers may choose to skip chapters or sections within chapters, or teach them in a different order, depending on student needs and time constraints. Each Student Book is self-contained so teachers may choose to use only one book, or the full series, if they wish.

Components at Each Level

- The **Student Book** is intended for classroom use and offers concise charts, level-appropriate explanations, and thorough four-skills practice exercises. Each Student Book is also a useful reference resource with extensive Appendices, a helpful Glossary of Grammar Terms, and a detailed Index.

- The **Audio Cassettes and CDs** feature listening exercises that provide practice discriminating form, understanding meaning and use, and interpreting non-standard forms.

- The **Workbook** has a wealth of additional exercises to supplement those in the Student Book. It is ideal for homework, independent practice, or review. The Answer Key, on easily removable perforated pages, is provided at the back of the book.

- The **Teacher's Book** has many practical ideas and techniques for presenting the Form and the Meaning and Use sections. It also includes troubleshooting advice, cultural notes, and suggestions for additional activities. The Answer Key for the Student Book and the complete Tapescript are also provided.

- **TOEFL®-Style Tests** and Answer Keys, along with advice on conducting the tests and interpreting the results, are available for teachers to download from the Internet. (See *Grammar Sense Teacher's Book 1* for the website address.)

Tour of a Chapter

Each chapter in *Grammar Sense* follows this format:

The **Grammar in Discourse** section introduces the target structure in its natural context via a high-interest authentic reading text.

> • *Authentic reading texts show how language is really used.*

> • *Structured reading tasks help students read and understand the text.*

The **Form** section(s) provides clear presentation of the target structure, detailed notes, and thorough practice exercises.

• Inductive **Examining Form** exercises encourage students to think about how to form the target structure.

FORM

B The Simple Past of *Be*

Examining Form

Look back at the excerpt on pages 170–171 and complete the tasks below. Then discuss your answers and read the Form charts to check them.

1. Look at the underlined examples of *be* in the simple past. Are they affirmative forms or negative forms? What are their subjects?

2. Look at the circled examples of *be* in the simple past. Are they affirmative forms or negative forms? Does the word *not* come before or after the verb?

3. Find four more affirmative examples of the simple past of *be*.

Affirmative Statements

SUBJECT	WAS/WERE	
I	**was**	
You	**were**	
He She It	**was**	helpful.
We		
You	**were**	
They		

Negative Statements

SUBJECT	WAS/WERE + NOT	
I	**was not wasn't**	
You	**were not weren't**	
He She It	**was not wasn't**	helpful.
We		
You	**were not weren't**	
They		

Yes/No Questions

WAS/WERE	SUBJECT	
Was	I	
Were	you	
Was	he she it	helpful?
Were	we you they	

Short Answers

YES	SUBJECT	WAS/WERE	NO	SUBJECT	WAS/WERE + NOT
	you	**were.**		you	**weren't.**
	I	**was.**		I	**wasn't.**
Yes,	he she it	**was.**	**No,**	he she it	**wasn't.**
	you			you	
	we	**were.**		we	**weren't.**
	they			they	

Information Questions

WH- WORD	WAS/WERE	SUBJECT	
Where	**was**	he	last week?
Why	**were**	you	in Hawaii?
What	**was**	that noise?	
When		we	in Boston?
Who	**were**	you	with?
How		the desserts?	

Answers

He **was** in London.
For Tom's wedding.
It was a barking dog.
In 1995.
My brother.
They **were** delicious!

172   Chapter 11 • Form

B3 Writing Affirmative and Negative Statements

The facts below are false. Correct each one by rewriting it as a negative statement. Then use the word or phrase in parentheses to write a true affirmative statement.

1. The pharaohs were generals. (kings)
   The pharaohs weren't generals. They were kings.

2. Cleopatra was a Persian general. (Egyptian queen)
   _____

3. Columbus was a lawyer. (explorer)
   _____

4. Picasso and Rembrandt were astronomers. (artists)
   _____

5. William Shakespeare was a French writer. (English)
   _____

6. Cervantes was an American inventor. (Spanish writer)
   _____

7. Marie Curie and Albert Einstein were doctors. (scientists)
   _____

8. Beethoven was a German king. (composer)
   _____

Form • The Simple Past of *Be*   175

• Clear and detailed **Form Charts** make learning the grammar easy.

• A wealth of exercises provide practice in manipulating the form.

The **Meaning and Use** section(s) offers clear and comprehensive explanations of how the target structure is used, and exercises to practice using it appropriately.

- *Inductive **Examining Meaning and Use** exercises encourage students to analyze how we use the target structure.*

MEANING AND USE

C The Simple Past of *Be*

Examining Meaning and Use

Read the sentences and answer the questions below. Then discuss your answers and read the Meaning and Use Notes to check them.

a. My uncle was a doctor.
b. The weather is rainy.
c. Yesterday the children were happy.
d. Twenty years ago he was a great athlete.
e. They weren't in Brazil last year.
f. Shakespeare was from England.

1. Which sentences show situations that existed in the past? Which show situations that exist in the present?

2. Which sentences use a word or phrase that tells you exactly when a situation existed in the past? Underline the word or phrase in each sentence.

Meaning and Use Notes

Common Uses of *Be* in the Simple Past

1 Use the simple past of *be* to talk about people, things, or situations that existed in the past.

Conditions
John and Sandra **were** sick yesterday.
Keisha **was** hungry.

Physical Characteristics
Last year Soon-jin's hair **was** long.
The school **was** small.

Occupations
Her brother **was** a taxi driver for four years.

Location and Origin
Those two new students **were** here yesterday.
Alexander the Great **was** from Macedonia.

(Continued on page 178)

178 Chapter 11 • Meaning and Use

Past Time Expressions

2 When we use the simple past of *be*, we often use a past time expression like *yesterday, last night/week/month*. We also use a period of time + *ago*. These past time expressions can occur at the beginning or end of a sentence.

I wasn't in school **yesterday**.
Last night they were at a party.
Irina's birthday was **ten days ago**.
The day before yesterday was Monday.
Last month we were in Argentina.
Five minutes ago Mike was in the kitchen.

C1 Listening for Meaning and Use   ▶ Note 1

Listen to each sentence. Is it about the past or the present? Check (✓) the correct column.

	PAST	PRESENT
1.	✓	
2.		
3.		
4.		
5.		
6.		

- *Succinct explanations and authentic examples illustrate the various meanings and uses of the structure.*

C4 Guessing About the Past   ▶ Note 1

Work with a partner. Think of a famous person from the past. Do not tell your partner the person's name. Take turns asking *Yes/No* questions about your partner's famous person. Try to guess the person's name.

A: *Was this person a man?*
B: *Yes, he was.*
A: *Was he an astronaut?*
B: *No, he wasn't.*
A: *Was he a scientist?*
B: *Yes, he was.*
A: *Is it Albert Einstein?*
B: *Yes, it is!*

C5 Talking About Your Past   ▶ Notes 1, 2

A. Work with a partner. Take turns asking and answering the following questions about your lives. Make notes about your partner's answers.

1. Where were you ten years ago?
2. Were you a student? If not, what were you?
3. What were you like?
4. What were your hobbies?
5. Who were your best friends?
6. What were your best friends like?

B. Change partners. Tell your new partner about your first partner. Use your notes.

Ten years ago Yuji was in Japan. He was a student in the sixth grade of elementary school. He was a good athlete. . .

C6 Describing Places in the Past   ▶ Note 1

A. What do you remember about your first school? Answer the questions.

1. Where was your first school?
2. How long were you a student there?
3. What was the school like?
4. Who was your favorite teacher?
5. What were your favorite lessons?
6. Were you a good student?

B. Write a paragraph describing your school. Use your answers in part A to guide you.

My first school was in Bogotá. I was a student there for six years. It was an old school with very big classrooms. My favorite teacher was Mr. Lopez. My favorite lessons were math, geography, and science. I was a good student.

180 Chapter 11 • Meaning and Use

- *Practice exercises enable students to use the structure appropriately and fluently.*

The **Review** section allows students to demonstrate their mastery of all aspects of the structure. It can be used for further practice or as a test.

● ***Thinking About Meaning and Use** exercises consolidate students' understanding of all aspects of the structure.*

● ***Editing** exercises teach students to correct their own writing.*

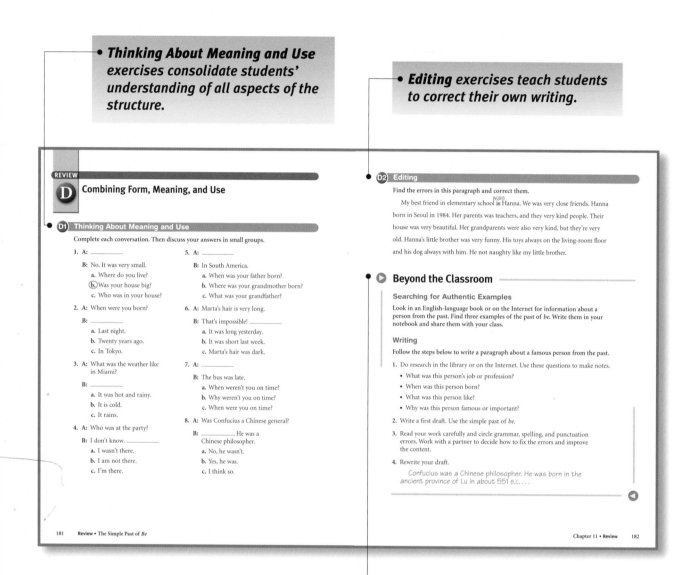

D Combining Form, Meaning, and Use

D1 Thinking About Meaning and Use

Complete each conversation. Then discuss your answers in small groups.

1. A: _____
   B: No. It was very small.
   a. Where do you live?
   (b.) Was your house big?
   c. Who was in your house?

2. A: When were you born?
   B: _____
   a. Last night.
   b. Twenty years ago.
   c. In Tokyo.

3. A: What was the weather like in Miami?
   B: _____
   a. It was hot and rainy.
   b. It is cold.
   c. It rains.

4. A: Who was at the party?
   B: I don't know. _____
   a. I wasn't there.
   b. I am not there.
   c. I'm there.

5. A: _____
   B: In South America.
   a. When was your father born?
   b. Where was your grandmother born?
   c. What was your grandfather?

6. A: Marta's hair is very long.
   B: That's impossible! _____
   a. It was long yesterday.
   b. It was short last week.
   c. Marta's hair was dark.

7. A: _____
   B: The bus was late.
   a. When weren't you on time?
   b. Why weren't you on time?
   c. When were you on time?

8. A: Was Confucius a Chinese general?
   B: _____. He was a Chinese philosopher.
   a. No, he wasn't.
   b. Yes, he was.
   c. I think so.

D2 Editing

Find the errors in this paragraph and correct them.

My best friend in elementary school ~~is~~ ^{was} Hanna. We was very close friends. Hanna born in Seoul in 1984. Her parents was teachers, and they very kind people. Their house was very beautiful. Her grandparents were also very kind, but they're very old. Hanna's little brother was very funny. His toys always on the living-room floor and his dog always with him. He not naughty like my little brother.

▶ **Beyond the Classroom**

Searching for Authentic Examples

Look in an English-language book or on the Internet for information about a person from the past. Find three examples of the past of *be*. Write them in your notebook and share them with your class.

Writing

Follow the steps below to write a paragraph about a famous person from the past.

1. Do research in the library or on the Internet. Use these questions to make notes.
   • What was this person's job or profession?
   • When was this person born?
   • What was this person like?
   • Why was this person famous or important?

2. Write a first draft. Use the simple past of *be*.

3. Read your work carefully and circle grammar, spelling, and punctuation errors. Work with a partner to decide how to fix the errors and improve the content.

4. Rewrite your draft.

   Confucius was a Chinese philosopher. He was born in the ancient province of Lu in about 551 B.C. . . .

● ***Beyond the Classroom** activities offer creative suggestions for further practice in new contexts.*

Special Sections appear throughout the chapters, with clear explanations, authentic examples, and follow-up exercises.

● *Pronunciation Notes* show students how to pronounce selected forms of the target language.

● *Beyond the Sentence* sections show how structures function differently in extended discourse.

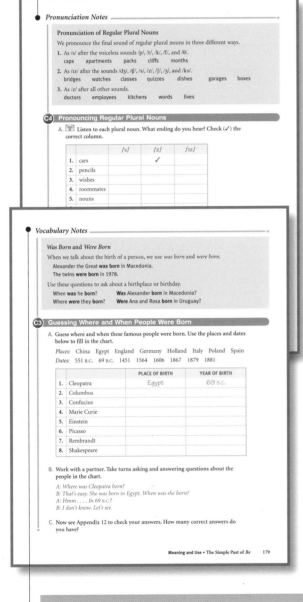

● *Pronunciation Notes*

Pronunciation of Regular Plural Nouns

We pronounce the final sound of regular plural nouns in three different ways.

1. As /s/ after the voiceless sounds /p/, /t/, /k/, /f/, and /θ/.
   caps   apartments   packs   cliffs   months

2. As /ɪz/ after the sounds /dʒ/, /tʃ/, /s/, /z/, /ʃ/, /ʒ/, and /ks/.
   bridges   watches   classes   quizzes   dishes   garages   boxes

3. As /z/ after all other sounds.
   doctors   employees   kitchens   words   lives

C4 **Pronouncing Regular Plural Nouns**

A. Listen to each plural noun. What ending do you hear? Check (✓) the correct column.

		/s/	/z/	/ɪz/
1.	cars		✓	
2.	pencils			
3.	wishes			
4.	roommates			
5.	nouns			

● *Vocabulary Notes*

Was Born and Were Born

When we talk about the birth of a person, we use *was born* and *were born*.

Alexander the Great **was born** in Macedonia.
The twins **were born** in 1978.

Use these questions to ask about a birthplace or birthday.

When **was** he **born**?   **Was** Alexander **born** in Macedonia?
Where **were** they **born**?   **Were** Ana and Rosa **born** in Uruguay?

C3 **Guessing Where and When People Were Born**

A. Guess where and when these famous people were born. Use the places and dates below to fill in the chart.

Places: China   Egypt   England   Germany   Holland   Italy   Poland   Spain
Dates: 551 B.C.   69 B.C.   1451   1564   1606   1867   1879   1881

		PLACE OF BIRTH	YEAR OF BIRTH
1.	Cleopatra	Egypt	69 B.C.
2.	Columbus		
3.	Confucius		
4.	Marie Curie		
5.	Einstein		
6.	Picasso		
7.	Rembrandt		
8.	Shakespeare		

B. Work with a partner. Take turns asking and answering questions about the people in the chart.

A: *Where was Cleopatra born?*
B: *That's easy. She was born in Egypt. When was she born?*
A: *Hmm . . . . In 69 B.C.?*
B: *I don't know. Let's see.*

C. Now see Appendix 12 to check your answers. How many correct answers do you have?

Meaning and Use • The Simple Past of *Be*   179

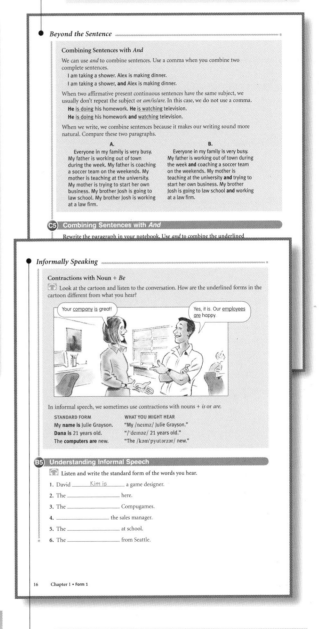

● *Beyond the Sentence*

Combining Sentences with *And*

We can use *and* to combine sentences. Use a comma when you combine two complete sentences.

I am taking a shower. Alex is making dinner.
I am taking a shower, **and** Alex is making dinner.

When two affirmative present continuous sentences have the same subject, we usually don't repeat the subject or *am/is/are*. In this case, we do not use a comma.

He is doing his homework. **He** is watching television.
He is doing his homework **and** watching television.

When we write, we combine sentences because it makes our writing sound more natural. Compare these two paragraphs.

A.	**B.**
Everyone in my family is very busy. My father is working out of town during the week. My father is coaching a soccer team on the weekends. My mother is teaching at the university. My mother is trying to start her own business. My brother Josh is going to law school. My brother Josh is working at a law firm.	Everyone in my family is very busy. My father is working out of town during the week **and** coaching a soccer team on the weekends. My mother is teaching at the university **and** trying to start her own business. My brother Josh is going to law school **and** working at a law firm.

C5 **Combining Sentences with *And***

Rewrite the paragraph in your notebook. Use *and* to combine the underlined

● *Informally Speaking*

Contractions with Noun + *Be*

Look at the cartoon and listen to the conversation. How are the underlined forms in the cartoon different from what you hear?

> Your company is great!

> Yes, it is. Our employees are happy.

In informal speech, we sometimes use contractions with nouns + *is* or *are*.

STANDARD FORM	WHAT YOU MIGHT HEAR
My name is Julie Grayson.	"My /neɪmz/ Julie Grayson."
Dana is 21 years old.	"/'deɪnəz/ 21 years old."
The computers are new.	"The /kəm'pyutərzər/ new."

B5 **Understanding Informal Speech**

Listen and write the standard form of the words you hear.

1. David ___Kim is___ a game designer.
2. The _____ here.
3. The _____ Compugames.
4. _____ the sales manager.
5. The _____ at school.
6. The _____ from Seattle.

16   Chapter 1 • Form 1

● *Vocabulary Notes* highlight the important connection between key vocabulary and grammatical structures.

● *Informally Speaking* sections show the differences between written and spoken language.

Before You Begin

Grammar Language

1 Nouns

▶ Nouns refer to people, animals, places, things, or ideas. To form the plural of many nouns, add -s.

A. Write the correct noun.

SINGULAR (one)	PLURAL (two or more)	SINGULAR (one)	PLURAL (two or more)

1. pencil   _pencils_

4. desk   _____

2. computer   _____

5. _____   calendars

3. _____   books

6. student   _____

B. Circle the correct noun.

1. two   chair /(chairs)   **3.** four   book / books   **5.** six   teacher / teachers

2. one   house / houses   **4.** three   pencil / pencils   **6.** a   girl / girls

2 Verbs

▶ Most verbs express actions. These verbs are called *action verbs*.

A. Read and follow the instructions.
1. **Work** with another student.
2. **Say** your full name to your partner.
3. **Write** your partner's full name on the line. _____
4. **Underline** your partner's first name.
5. **Circle** your partner's family name.

▶ Some verbs do not express actions. They express states or conditions such as feelings, mental states, or physical states. These verbs are called *stative verbs*.

B. Write *A* for action verb or *S* for stative verb for each statement.

   _A_   1. We **eat** in the cafeteria.   _____   4. **Write** your name.

   _____   2. The chairs **are** small.   _____   5. **Close** the door.

   _____   3. I **feel** sick.   _____   6. We **are** students.

C. Look at the words. Underline the verbs.

<u>say</u>   desk   pencil   word   sit   am   girl   read

3 Adjectives

▶ Adjectives describe nouns.

Look at the pictures. Match the phrases to the pictures.

A.   **B.**

   _A_   1. a **white** car   _____   3. a **big** car   _____   5. an **expensive** car

   _____   2. a **black** car   _____   4. a **small** car   _____   6. a **cheap** car

▶ Prepositions tell direction, origin, location, or time.

A. Study the picture. Then read the sentences below.

Class is **at** 8:00.

The flowers are **in** the vase.

The book is **on** the desk.

The bag is **under** the desk.

The teacher is **next to** the desk.

Betty Lin is **from** China.

B. Work with a partner. Describe things in your classroom. Use *in, on, next to,* and *under.*

The pencil is on the desk.

C. Read the sentences. Look at the underlined words. Write *A* for adjective or *P* for preposition above each word.

1. The A
new movie is P
at 1:30.

2. John is in the red car.

3. The student from Japan is young.

4. Put the dirty dishes next to the sink.

5. The paper is under the green book.

6. The expensive shop is on the corner.

▶ Pronouns replace nouns. A subject pronoun comes before the verb in a sentence.

A. Study the pictures.

SINGULAR SUBJECT PRONOUNS

PLURAL SUBJECT PRONOUNS

B. Complete the sentences with subject pronouns.

1. Mrs. Harris is a teacher. _She_ is a good teacher.

2. Juan is in the car. _____ is in the blue car.

3. Mr. and Mrs. Welch are Americans. _____ are from New York.

4. The chair is new. _____ is not old.

5. You and your friend are new students. _____ are in my class.

6. Derek and I are students. _____ are in college.

The Verb *Be* and Imperatives

Simple Present Statements with *Be*

A | ## Meet the Staff

A1 | ### Before You Read

Discuss these questions.

Do you work or study? What is your job? What do you study? Do you like it?

A2 | ### Read

Read these conversations. Who is Carol?

Carol: Mr. Goodrich?

John: Sorry. Mike Goodrich isn't at work today. I'm his assistant. My name is John Louis.

Carol: My name is Carol Cheng. I'm a new employee.

John: Of course! You're the new sales manager.

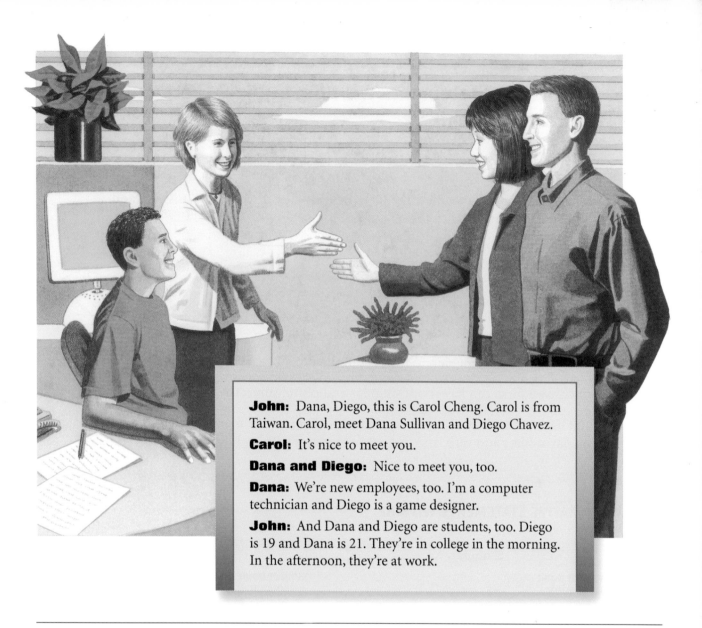

John: Dana, Diego, this is Carol Cheng. Carol is from Taiwan. Carol, meet Dana Sullivan and Diego Chavez.

Carol: It's nice to meet you.

Dana and Diego: Nice to meet you, too.

Dana: We're new employees, too. I'm a computer technician and Diego is a game designer.

John: And Dana and Diego are students, too. Diego is 19 and Dana is 21. They're in college in the morning. In the afternoon, they're at work.

---

assistant: a helper

computer technician: a person who fixes computers

employee: a person who works for a company

game designer: a person who makes new games

sales manager: a head of a sales department

A3 After You Read

Match each person to his or her job.

 _b_ **1.** John Louis   **a.** game designer

 ____ **2.** Carol Cheng   **b.** assistant

 ____ **3.** Dana Sullivan   **c.** sales manager

 ____ **4.** Diego Chavez   **d.** computer technician

B Affirmative Statements with *Be*, Subject Pronouns, and Contractions with *Be*

Examining Form

Read the sentences and complete the tasks below. Then discuss your answers and read the Form charts to check them.

> **a.** I am a new employee.
> **b.** Dana and Diego are new employees, too.
> **c.** Carol is from Taiwan.
> **d.** You are the new sales manager.

1. Circle the subjects and underline the verbs.

2. Which subjects are singular? Which is plural? Which subjects are pronouns?

3. Which verb form can have both singular and plural subjects?

4. Look back at the conversations on pages 10–11. Find one more sentence with a singular subject and verb, and one more sentence with a plural subject and verb.

AFFIRMATIVE STATEMENTS WITH *BE*

Singular			Plural		
SUBJECT NOUN or PRONOUN	*BE*		**SUBJECT NOUN or PRONOUN**	*BE*	
I	am	an employee.	**Dana** and **I** / We	are	employees.
You	are	young.	**You** and **Diego** / You	are	young.
Diego / He	is	in college.	**Diego** and **Dana** / They	are	in college.
Dana / She					
Compugames / It	is	a company.	**Compugames** and **DSL** / They	are	companies.

Singular	
SUBJECT PRONOUN + *BE*	CONTRACTION
I am	I**'m**
You are	You**'re**
He is	He**'s**
She is	She**'s**
It is	It**'s**

Plural	
SUBJECT PRONOUN + *BE*	CONTRACTION
We are	We**'re**
You are	You**'re**
They are	They**'re**

Affirmative Statements with *Be*

- Every sentence has a subject and a verb. The subject is a noun or pronoun.
- The verb *be* has three present tense forms: *am, is, are.*

Subject Pronouns and Contractions with *Be*

- The singular subject pronouns are *I, you, he, she, it.* The plural subject pronouns are *we, you, they.*
- Use *it* for things and animals. Sometimes we use *he* or *she* for animals.
- A contraction with *be* combines a subject pronoun and the verb *be.* An apostrophe (') replaces the missing letters of the verb (**I'm** = I am).
- You can use contractions with *be* in speaking and writing.

B1 Listening for Form

🎧 Carol and John are employees at Compugames. Listen to their statements. What form of *be* do you hear in each sentence? Check (✓) the correct column.

	AM OR '*M*	*IS* OR '*S*	*ARE* OR '*RE*
1.		✓	
2.			
3.			
4.			
5.			
6.			
7.			
8.			

B2) Working on Affirmative Statements

Complete the paragraph with *am, is,* or *are.*

My name ____is____ Mike Goodrich. I _____ the president of
Compugames. Compugames _____ an Internet videogame company. Our
employees _____ from all over the world. I _____ from Seattle. Celia
Rivera _____ the vice president of Compugames. She _____ from
Puerto Rico. Ruth McMaster and Carol Cheng _____ two new employees.
Ruth _____ from New York, and Carol _____ from Taiwan. Diego and
Dana _____ new employees. They _____ also college students.

B3) Working on Pronouns and Contractions

A. Complete the sentences. Use subject pronoun + *be* contractions.

1. Mr. Walsh is our computer technician. __He's__ from Canada.

2. Compugames is a company. _____ in Seattle.

3. Mark and Pete are new employees. _____ game designers.

4. Ana and I are students. _____ from Mexico.

5. Some employees are in college. _____ busy.

6. My name is Hiro. _____ from Japan.

7. Carol is at work. _____ a sales manager.

8. You and Donna are new employees. _____ in my department.

9. *Rocket Race* is our new video game. _____ fun!

10. Our offices are on Jackson Street. _____ big.

B. Work with a partner. Take turns saying the sentences with contractions
in part A.

He's from Canada.

Complete the conversations. Add *am, is,* or *are* in the correct place. Use contractions with pronouns when possible.

Conversation 1: At the office

John: My name ^is John Lucas.

Sara: Hi, John. I Sara Walker.

John: Oh, you the new game designer. Welcome!

Sara: Thank you. It nice to meet you.

John: It nice to meet you, too.

Conversation 2: On campus

Beth: Steve, this my roommate, Lisa.

Steve: Hi, Lisa.

Beth: Steve, you from California. Lisa from California, too.

Steve: Really? I from San Francisco.

Lisa: I from San Diego.

(Lisa and Beth leave.)

Lisa: Steve handsome!

Beth: Yes. And he nice, too.

Conversation 3: At a party

Rosa: Jenny and I computer technicians at ElectroDesign.

Juan: Oh! You lucky!

Rosa: Yes, ElectroDesign a great company.

Jenny: The employees very happy.

Juan: My sons computer technicians, too. They employees at Reed.

Contractions with Noun + *Be*

🎧 Look at the cartoon and listen to the conversation. How are the underlined forms in the cartoon different from what you hear?

> Your <u>company is</u> great!

> Yes, it is. Our <u>employees are</u> happy.

In informal speech, we sometimes use contractions with nouns + *is* or *are*.

STANDARD FORM	WHAT YOU MIGHT HEAR
My **name is** Julie Grayson.	"My /neɪmz/ Julie Grayson."
Dana is 21 years old.	"/ˈdeɪnəz/ 21 years old."
The **computers are** new.	"The /kəmˈpyutərzər/ new."

B5 ### Understanding Informal Speech

🎧 Listen and write the standard form of the words you hear.

1. David _____*Kim is*_____ a game designer.

2. The _____ here.

3. The _____ Compugames.

4. _____ the sales manager.

5. The _____ at school.

6. The _____ from Seattle.

C Negative Statements and Contractions with *Be*

Examining Form

Read the sentences and complete the tasks below. Then discuss your answers and read the Form charts to check them.

1a. He is not here.
1b. They are not small.

2a. He isn't here.
2b. They aren't small.

3a. He's not here.
3b. They're not small.

1. Look at sentences 1a and 1b. Underline the verb in each sentence. Is *not* before or after the verb?

2. Underline the contractions of *be* + *not* in 2a and 2b. How are they different?

3. Circle the contractions of subject + *be* before *not* in 3a and 3b. How are they different?

NEGATIVE STATEMENTS WITH *BE*

Singular			
SUBJECT	BE	NOT	
I	am		
You	are		
He She	is	not	a game designer.
It	is		a new company.

Plural			
SUBJECT	BE	NOT	
We			
You			
They	are	not	game designers.
They			new companies.

- Add *not* after *be* to make a sentence negative.

(Continued on page 18)

Singular	
SUBJECT PRONOUN + *BE* + *NOT*	CONTRACTION
I am not	I**'m not**
You are not	You **aren't** You**'re not**
He is not	He **isn't** He**'s not**
She is not	She **isn't** She**'s not**
It is not	It **isn't** It**'s not**

Plural	
SUBJECT PRONOUN + *BE* + *NOT*	CONTRACTION
We are not	We **aren't** We**'re not**
You are not	You **aren't** You**'re not**
They are not	They **aren't** They**'re not**

- *Am not* has only one contracted form.
- *Are not* and *is not* have two different contracted forms.
- You can use negative contractions with *be* in speaking and writing.

C1 **Listening for Form**

Listen to each sentence. Is the sentence affirmative or negative? Check (✓) the correct column.

	AFFIRMATIVE	NEGATIVE
1.	✓	
2.		
3.		
4.		
5.		
6.		
7.		
8.		

C2) Forming Negative Statements

Form negative statements with the words and phrases. Use contractions when possible. Punctuate your sentences correctly. Compare them with a partner.

1. in California/not/Seattle/is

   Seattle isn't in California.

2. is/Larry/not/from France

   _____

3. Lisa and I/not/students/are

   _____

4. big/our school/is/not

   _____

5. am/I/not/Canadian

   _____

6. in my class/are/not/you

   _____

C3) Working on Pronouns and Negative Contractions

Rewrite the sentences using subject pronouns and contractions. Use two different contracted forms.

1. Sara is not happy.

   She's not happy.

   She isn't happy.

2. Bob is not a manager.

   _____

   _____

3. You and Steve are not teachers.

   _____

   _____

4. The school is not big.

   _____

   _____

5. Rick and Yuki are not in class.

   _____

   _____

6. Eva and I are not Italian.

   _____

   _____

A. Complete the conversations with negative forms of *be*. Use contractions when possible.

Conversation 1

A: Hello. I'm a new student here.

B: __I'm not__ the teacher. He _____ here.
　　　　　1　　　　　　　　　　　　2

Conversation 2

A: Your pens are on the table.

B: No, they _____. My pens _____ blue. They're black.
　　　　　　　　1　　　　　　　　　　　　2

Conversation 3

A: Marta _____ in class.
　　　　　　　　1

B: That's right. She and her sister _____ in school today. They're sick.
　　　　　　　　　　　　　　　　　　　2

Conversation 4

A: Hurry! Your class is at 12:00. It's 12:10. You're late.

B: I _____ late. My class _____ at 12:00. It's at 1:00.
　　　　　1　　　　　　　　　　　2

Conversation 5

A: Your computer is very fast.

B: It _____ my computer. My computer _____ very fast at all.
　　　　　1　　　　　　　　　　　　　　　　　　2

Conversation 6

A: Carla and Roberta _____ in the office today.
　　　　　　　　　　　　　1

B: No, they _____. They're at a meeting.
　　　　　　　　2

B. Practice the conversations in part A with a partner.

A: Hello. I'm a new student here.
B: I'm not the teacher. . . .

D Descriptions with *Be*

Examining Meaning and Use

Read the sentences and answer the questions below. Then discuss your answers and read the Meaning and Use Notes to check them.

a. David is 25 years old.   **c.** She is sick.
b. I am from Mexico.   **d.** Mr. Grant is a teacher.

Which sentence talks about someone's:

____ health?   ____ age?   ____ job?   ____ country?

Meaning and Use Notes

Conditions and Characteristics

1 Use *be* with adjectives to describe conditions, physical characteristics, age, and personality.

Condition	*Physical Characteristic*	*Age*	*Personality*
Jada **is sick.**	The school **is big.**	Josh **is ten (years old).**	Lee **is friendly.**

Identifying and Describing Nouns

2 Use *be* with nouns to identify or define something, describe occupations, and describe relationships.

Identifying	*Describing Occupations*	*Describing Relationships*
It**'s a map.**	He**'s a game designer.**	Lisa **is my friend.**

Location and Origin

3A Use *be* with prepositions to describe location (where people or things are). We also use words such as *here, there, upstairs,* and *downstairs.*
She**'s not in class.** She**'s at home.**   They**'re not here.** They**'re upstairs.**

3B Use *be* with prepositions or adjectives to describe origin (the country where people or things are from).

With Prepositions: They**'re from Chile.**   *With Adjectives:* They**'re Chilean.**

(Continued on page 22)

Talking About Time, Dates, and Weather

4 We use *it* with *be* for the time, the day/date, and the weather.

Time	*Day*	*Weather*
It's eight o'clock.	**It's** Thursday.	**It's** cold and windy.

D1 Listening for Meaning and Use   ▶ Notes 1–3B

🎧 Listen to each sentence. Does it describe an age or characteristic, an occupation, or a location or origin? Check (✓) the correct column.

	AGE OR CHARACTERISTIC	OCCUPATION	LOCATION OR ORIGIN
1.			✓
2.			
3.			
4.			
5.			
6.			

D2 Defining and Describing Nouns   ▶ Note 2

A. Complete the definitions using the words below.

colors   Europe   fruits   pizza
dictionary   flower   June   Rome and Venice

1. _Europe_ is a continent.

2. A daisy is a _____.

3. _____ are cities.

4. Green and yellow are _____.

5. A _____ is a book

6. Apples and oranges are _____.

7. _____ is a month.

8. _____ is Italian.

B. Write four more sentences using some of these words.

animal   colors   countries   flower   language   months

Brazil and Peru are countries in South America.

Work with a partner. Look at the pictures. Write one affirmative and one negative statement in your notebook with the words below.

beautiful   big   old   small   ugly   young

1.

3.

5.

He's old. He isn't young.

2.

4.

6.

Complete the conversations with a time, a date, or the weather.

1. **A:** The weather is beautiful

   B: Yes, _it's warm and sunny_____.

2. **A:** We are late! It's 3:00.

   B: We are not late. _____.

3. **A:** It's late in New York. It's 11:00 P.M.

   B: _____ in Los Angeles.

4. **A:** Oh no! The bank is closed.

   B: Of course, it's closed. _____.

5. **A:** When is your birthday?

   B: _____

Introduce yourself to three classmates. Include your name, age, country of origin, and occupation.

A: *My name is Kathy Lim. I'm 22 years old. I'm from Korea. I'm a student.*
B: *Nice to meet you, Kathy. My name is . . .*

Beyond the Sentence

Using Pronouns in Paragraphs

In paragraphs the first time we talk about the subject of a sentence we use a subject noun. After that, we often use the subject pronoun form to refer to the same noun.

Read the paragraphs below. Notice how the pronouns make the second paragraph more interesting.

Paragraph with No Pronouns

Carol Cheng is from Taiwan. Carol is a new employee at Compugames. Carol is the sales manager. Compugames is a videogame company. Compugames is a new company. Compugames is in Seattle.

Paragraph with Pronouns

Carol Cheng is from Taiwan. **She**'s a new employee at Compugames. **She**'s the sales manager. Compugames is a videogame company. **It**'s a new company. **It**'s in Seattle.

D6 **Using Pronouns in Paragraphs**

Rewrite the paragraph. Use pronouns to replace some of the nouns.

Sally is 17 years old. Sally is not a normal teenager. In the afternoon Sally is an employee at Macro Ads. Sally is not the only teenager there. Mark is an employee, too. Mark is only 16 years old. Both teenagers are students at West Valley High School. West Valley High School is near the offices of Macro Ads.

<u> Sally is 17 years old. She . . . </u>

_____

_____

_____

E # Combining Form, Meaning, and Use

Complete each sentence. Then discuss your answers in small groups.

1. John is an employee at Compugames.

_____ is an assistant.

   a. She

   (b.) He

   c. It

2. Pedro is from the Dominican Republic.

He _____ from Puerto Rico.

   a. is

   b. are

   c. isn't

3. Lynn and I are game designers. We

_____ sales managers.

   a. isn't

   b. am not

   c. are not

4. Bangkok is a large city. _____

is the capital of Thailand.

   a. It

   b. He

   c. She

5. The company is new. _____ old.

   a. They're

   b. They aren't

   c. It isn't

6. Brazil _____ in North America.

   a. not

   b. is not

   c. is no

Some of these sentences have errors. Find the errors and correct them.

1. Lucy ~~am~~ a teacher. *(is)*

2. India in Asia.

3. We are at home.

4. She in the classroom.

5. They happy.

6. I amn't a student.

7. Paulo no is Brazilian.

8. You're not in my English class.

Beyond the Classroom

Searching for Authentic Examples

Look at English-language books and newspapers, or on the Internet. Find examples of subject pronouns + *be*. Write them in your notebook. What is the noun that the subject pronoun replaces? Share the sentences with your class.

Writing

Reread the paragraph in exercise D6 on page 24. Then follow these steps to write a paragraph about someone you know.

1. Use the form below to make notes.

Someone I Know

Name: _____

Age: _____

Country: _____

School or Company: _____

Job: _____

Other: _____

---

2. Write a first draft. Use affirmative and negative statements with the correct form of *be*.

3. Read your work carefully and circle grammar, spelling, and punctuation errors. Work with a partner to decide how to fix the errors and improve the content.

4. Rewrite your draft.

> Mark Hunter is my best friend. He is 20 years old. He is from England. Mark is in college. In the afternoons, he is a salesperson.

Questions with *Be*

A Are You Best Friends?

A1 **Before You Read**

Discuss these questions.

Do you have many good friends? Are your good friends similar to you? Describe your best friend.

A2 **Read**

🎧 **Read this conversation and the magazine quiz about friends on the following page. Then take the quiz. Are you and your best friend similar?**

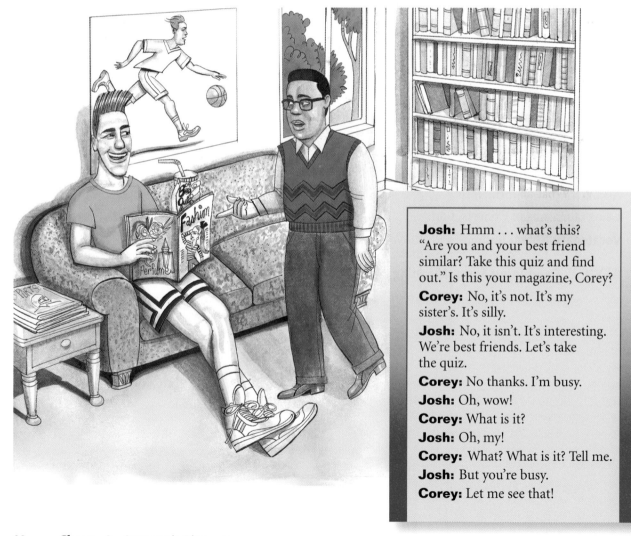

Josh: Hmm . . . what's this? "Are you and your best friend similar? Take this quiz and find out." Is this your magazine, Corey?

Corey: No, it's not. It's my sister's. It's silly.

Josh: No, it isn't. It's interesting. We're best friends. Let's take the quiz.

Corey: No thanks. I'm busy.

Josh: Oh, wow!

Corey: What is it?

Josh: Oh, my!

Corey: What? What is it? Tell me.

Josh: But you're busy.

Corey: Let me see that!

Are You Best Friends?

Are you and your best friend similar? Are you different?
Are you really best friends?
Take this quiz and find out.

Who is your best friend? _____

	YOU	Yes	No	YOUR BEST FRIEND	Yes	No
1.	Are you a social person?			Is your best friend a social person?		
2.	Are you a private person?			Is your best friend a private person?		
3.	Are you a good student?			Is your best friend a good student?		
4.	Are you cautious?			Is your best friend cautious?		
5.	Are you athletic?			Is your best friend athletic?		
6.	Are you active?			Is your best friend active?		
7.	Are you a spendthrift?			Is your best friend a spendthrift?		
8.	What is your favorite kind of music? _____ _____			What is your best friend's favorite kind of music? _____ _____		
9.	What are your hobbies? _____ _____			What are your best friend's hobbies? _____ _____		

active: busy
athletic: having a strong, healthy body
cautious: careful
find out: to learn or discover

private: not sharing feelings
social: having many friends
silly: not serious
spendthrift: a person who spends a lot of money

A3 After You Read

Work in small groups. Compare your answers to the magazine quiz.

B Yes/No Questions and Short Answers with Be

Examining Form

Read the sentences and complete the tasks below. Then discuss your answers and read the Form charts to check them.

a. It's silly.
b. Are you best friends?
c. Is she athletic?
d. Yes, they are.
e. We're best friends.
f. No, it isn't.

1. Which sentences are statements? Which are questions?

2. Circle the subjects and underline the verbs.

3. In statements, which is first, the subject or the verb? Which is first in questions?

Yes/No Questions with *Be*		
BE	**SUBJECT**	
Am	I	
Are	you	
Is	he	
	she	late?
	it	
Are	we	
	you	
	they	

Short Answers				
YES	**SUBJECT**	**BE**	**NO**	**SUBJECT + BE + NOT**
	you	are.		you **aren't**. you**'re not**.
	I	am.		I**'m not**.
	he	is.		he **isn't**. he**'s not**.
Yes,	she	is.	**No,**	she **isn't**. she**'s not**.
	it	is.		it **isn't**. it**'s not**.
	you	are.		you **aren't**. you**'re not**.
	we	are.		we **aren't**. we**'re not**.
	they	are.		they **aren't**. they**'re not**.

Yes/No Questions

- In a question, *be* comes before the subject. A question ends with a question mark *(?)*.

Statement	Yes/No *Question*
They **are** late.	**Are they** late?

- Use a singular form of *be* with singular subjects. Use the plural form of *be* with plural subjects.

Singular	Plural
Is he late?	**Are** we late?

Short Answers

- We usually answer *Yes/No* questions with short answers.

- Do not use contractions in short answers with *yes*.

  Yes, **I am.**   * Yes, I'm. (INCORRECT)

B1 **Listening for Form**

Listen to each sentence. Is it a question or a statement? Check (✓) the correct column.

	QUESTION	STATEMENT
1.	✓	
2.		
3.		
4.		
5.		
6.		
7.		
8.		
9.		
10.		

A. Form *Yes/No* questions. Use the words and phrases. Punctuate your sentences correctly.

1. from the United States/your best friend/is

   Is your best friend from the United States?

2. you/a smoker/are

   _____

3. your family/is/in the United States

   _____

4. your English/is/good

   _____

5. you/are/an active person

   _____

6. big/is/your home

   _____

B. Work with a partner. Take turns asking and answering the questions in part A.

A: Is your best friend from the United States?
B: No, she isn't.

B3) Changing Statements into Questions

Change the statements into *Yes/No* questions. Write them in your notebook. Use the correct pronoun in place of the subject noun.

1. Paul is from Saratoga Springs.
   Is he from Saratoga Springs?

2. Your English class is interesting.

3. Linda and Paul are friends.

4. Mrs. Miller is a Spanish teacher.

5. Juan and I are late for the party.

6. Emily is a spendthrift.

C Information Questions with *Be*

Examining Form

Read the sentences and complete the tasks below. Then discuss your answers and read the Form charts to check them.

1a. How is Marcia? **2a.** Where are the classes?
1b. Is Marcia sick? **2b.** Are the classes here?

1. Which questions are *Yes/No* questions? Which are information questions? What words do the information questions begin with?

2. Circle the subjects and underline the verbs in each question. Is the order of the subject and the verb the same in all of the questions?

Information Questions			Answers
WH- WORD	*BE*	SUBJECT	
Where	**am**	I?	On the second floor. You**'re** on the second floor.
How	**are**	you?	Fine, thanks. I**'m** fine, thanks.
Who	**is**	he?	My roommate. He**'s** my roommate.
		she?	My sister. She**'s** my sister.
When		it?	At noon. It**'s** at noon.
Where	**are**	we?	On Main Street. You**'re** on Main Street.
		you?	On campus. We**'re** on campus.
What		they?	Shoes. They**'re** shoes.

(Continued on page 34)

- Information questions are similar to *Yes/No* questions, but they begin with a question word (*wh-* word). The question word is before *be*.

  Yes/No *Question*   *Information Question*

  Is the manager outside?   **Where** is the manager?

- Use a singular form of *be* with singular subjects. Use a plural form of *be* with plural subjects.

- It is not necessary to answer an information question with a complete sentence.

C1 Listening for Form

🎧 **Listen to each question in the conversation. Is it a *Yes/No* question or an information question? Check (✓) the correct column.**

	YES/NO QUESTION	INFORMATION QUESTION
1.	✓	
2.		
3.		
4.		
5.		
6.		

C2 Changing Statements into Questions

Change the statements into information questions. Use the question word in parentheses. Punctuate your sentences correctly.

1. My name is Julie Bishop. (what) _What is your name?_

2. The apartment is very nice. (how) _____

3. The appointment is at 8:00. (when) _____

4. The apartment is on Carson Street. (where) _____

5. Mrs. Hewitt is the manager. (who) _____

6. Jada and Emily are the other roommates. (who) _____

Contractions with *Wh-* Word + *Be*

🎧 Look at the cartoon and listen to the conversation. How is the underlined form in the cartoon different from what you hear?

How are the students?

They're great!

In informal speech, we often use contractions with question words + *is* or *are*.

STANDARD FORM	WHAT YOU MIGHT HEAR
When is the class?	"/wɛnz/ the class?"
How is your apartment?	"/haʊz/ your apartment?"
Who are your roommates?	"/huər/ your roommates?"
What are their jobs?	"/ˈwʌtər/ their jobs?"
Where are the students?	"/ˈwɛrər/ the students?"
How are your teachers?	"/ˈhaʊər/ your teachers?"
When are the tests?	"/ˈwɛnər/ the tests?"

C3 Understanding Informal Speech

🎧 **Listen and write the standard form of the words you hear.**

1. <u>Where are</u> the children?

2. _____ their names?

3. _____ the meal?

4. _____ your friends?

5. _____ your class?

6. _____ your roommate?

7. _____ your grades?

8. _____ your books?

D Questions with *Be*

Examining Meaning and Use

Read the sentences and answer the questions below. Then discuss your answers and read the Meaning and Use Notes to check them.

1a. **Bob:** Is Fumiko from China?   2a. **Jane:** Where is Fumiko from?
1b. **Sara:** No, she isn't.   2b. **Dan:** She's from Japan.

1. Look at the questions and answers above. Which question asks if something is true or not?

2. Which question asks for specific information?

3. Which answer gives more information?

Meaning and Use Notes

Asking If Something Is True

1 Use *Yes/No* questions to find out if information is true or not.

A: **Are** you from Mexico?   A: **Is** your math class difficult?   A: **Is** Istanbul in Italy?
B: Yes, I am.   B: Yes, it is.   B: No, it's not.

A: **Is** Betty your friend?   A: **Is** breakfast at 8:00?
B: Yes, she is.   B: Yes, it is.

Asking for New Information

 2A Use information questions when you want to learn specific information about someone or something.

A: **Where** are you from?   A: **How** is your math class?   A: **Where** is Istanbul?
B: Mexico.   B: It's very difficult!   B: In Turkey.

A: **Who** is your friend?   A: **When** is breakfast?
B: Betty Brown.   B: At 8:00.

2B Use *wh-* words to ask for specific information.

Who *for People*
A: **Who is** your teacher?
B: Mr. Brown.

Where *for Places*
A: **Where are** you from?
B: Argentina.

How *for Conditions*
A: **How are** you?
B: Fine, thanks.

What *for Things*
A: **What's** that?
B: It's my new phone.

When *for Time*
A: **When is** the test?
B: Tomorrow.

How *for Opinions*
A: **How are** your classes?
B: They're interesting.

Using Questions in Conversation

3 *Yes/No* questions and answers are usually short and direct. Ask an information question when you want to have a longer conversation with someone.

Yes/No Question
A: **Is** your roommate from Korea?
B: No.

Information Questions
A: **Where** is your roommate from?
B: She's from Taiwan. Her name's Jenny Wang.
A: My roommate is from Taiwan, too!
B: Really? **What's** his name?
A: David Wang. Maybe he's Jenny's brother!

D1 **Listening for Meaning and Use**   ► Notes 1–2B

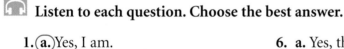 **Listen to each question. Choose the best answer.**

1. **(a.)** Yes, I am.
   b. I'm a student.

2. **a.** No, it isn't.
   b. Business.

3. **a.** Yes, it is.
   b. I'm at the university.

4. **a.** No, I'm not.
   b. It's beautiful.

5. **a.** Yes, I am.
   b. I'm from New York.

6. **a.** Yes, they are.
   b. They're in my class.

7. **a.** Yes, she is.
   b. Mrs. Jenkins.

8. **a.** Yes, she is.
   b. She's in her office.

9. **a.** I'm in the dorm.
   b. South Dorm.

10. **a.** No, it's not.
    b. It's small.

Work with a partner. Look at the picture. Ask and answer *Yes/No* **questions.**
Use the words and phrases.

1. keys/on the floor

   A: Are the keys on the floor?
   B: No, they aren't

2. Julia/athletic

3. windows/open

4. Julia/happy

5. Julia/bad student

6. the shelf/neat

7. the ball/on the bed

8. the room/messy

D3 **Asking for New Information** ► Notes 2A, 2B

A. **Complete the form with your information.**

1. Name:

2. Address:

3. Country:

4. Hobbies:

5. Best friend:

6. Birthday:

B. Write questions about the information on the form on the previous page. Use the *wh-* words below. Punctuate your sentences correctly.

1. What <u>is your name?</u>

2. What _____

3. Where _____

4. What _____

5. Who _____

6. When _____

C. Work with a partner. Use the information on your form to ask and answer questions.

A: What is your name?
B: My name is Elena Karanova.

D4 **Contrasting *Yes/No* and Information Questions** ► Notes 1–3

Complete the conversation with appropriate questions. Punctuate your sentences correctly.

Pete: Chris, meet Jorge Zapata. He's our new roommate.

Chris: Hi Jorge. <u>Where are you from?</u>
  1

Jorge: I'm from Mexico.

Chris: Wow! _____
           2

Jorge: No, I'm not from Mexico City. I'm from Monterrey.

Pete: _____
          3

Jorge: Yes, it is. It's very hot in Monterrey. . . . This apartment is very nice.

_____
          4

Pete: No, it isn't. The neighborhood is very quiet.

Jorge: Great. _____
                   5

Chris: The stores are on Freeman Street.

Jorge: _____
           6

Pete: The buses are great. They aren't crowded and they're on time.

Vocabulary Notes

Responses to *Yes/No* Questions

We use several different responses to *Yes/No* questions. These responses express different levels of certainty and formality.

	FORMAL	INFORMAL
Certainty	Yes. / No.	Yeah. / Yep. / Nope.
Some Certainty	I think so. / I don't think so. I'm not sure. Perhaps. Maybe.	I think so. / I don't think so. I'm not sure. Maybe.
Uncertainty	I don't know.	Don't know. You got me. I have no idea.

D5 Responding to *Yes/No* Questions

A. Imagine a conversation with the following people. Write *F* if the situation is formal. Write *I* if it is informal.

___F___ **1.** your teacher _____ **4.** a police officer

_____ **2.** your friend _____ **5.** your new landlord

_____ **3.** your brother or sister _____ **6.** your boss

B. Work with a partner. Imagine you are the people in each situation. Take turns asking and answering the questions. Use appropriate responses from the Vocabulary Notes.

1. **Landlord:** Is your heat broken?
   Tenant: _I think so._

2. **Teacher:** Is Lusaka the capital of Namibia?
   Student: _____

3. **Guest:** Is it cold in Jakarta?
   Hotel clerk: _____

4. **Brother:** Is your teacher nice?
   Sister: _____

5. **Boss:** Is the meeting in Room 5?
   Employee: _____

6. **Friend:** Is English class interesting?
   Friend: _____

E Combining Form, Meaning, and Use

E1 Thinking About Meaning and Use

Complete each conversation. Then discuss your answers in small groups.

1. A: _____

   B: No, it's in the library.
      a. How is the class?
      b. Is the class here? ⟵ (circled)

2. A: Where is Linda?

   B: _____
      a. In class.
      b. An engineer.

3. A: When is dinner?

   B: _____
      a. Very nice.
      b. It's at 6:00.

4. A: _____

   B: A new student.
      a. Who is he?
      b. How is he?

5. A: Who are they?

   B: _____
      a. Alex and Naomi.
      b. They're fine.

6. A: _____

   B: No, they aren't.
      a. Where are they?
      b. Are they home?

7. A: _____

   B: It's interesting.
      a. How is the book?
      b. Where is the book?

8. A: _____

   B: It's at 9:30.
      a. Where is your appointment?
      b. When is your appointment?

9. A: _____

   B: She's from Japan.
      a. Where is Keiko from?
      b. Who is Keiko?

10. A: When is the class?

    B: _____
       a. Yes, it is.
       b. At 3:00.

Some of these sentences have errors. Find the errors and correct them.

1. Where ~~she is~~? *is she*

2. Is happy the teacher?

3. Where Dana is?

4. Who they?

5. When is the meeting?

6. How you are?

7. Yes, I'm.

8. She 19 years old.

▶ Beyond the Classroom

Searching for Authentic Examples

Watch an English-language movie or TV program. Listen for examples of *Yes/No* questions and information questions with *be*. Write three Y*es/No* questions and three information questions with answers in your notebook. Share them with your class.

Speaking

Follow the steps below to prepare an interview for a new roommate.

1. Write six interview questions. Use *Yes/No* and information questions.

2. Bring your questions to class. Work with a partner and ask your partner the interview questions. Write down your partner's answers.

   A: Are you a student?
   B: Yes, I am.

3. Change partners two more times and ask your new partners the same interview questions.

4. Tell the class which partner is the best roommate for you.

Imperatives

A The Adventures of an Office Assistant

A1 Before You Read

Discuss these questions.

What is an office assistant? Is it a good job? Why or why not?

A2 Read

 Read these conversations. Is Rob busy at his new job?

> **Mr. Brooks:** Rob, please bring this contract to Mr. Douglas. It's very important.
>
> **Ms. Lopez:** Rob, take this to the mailroom immediately. Do not forget.
>
> **Mr. Green:** Rob, call Snyder Supply Company for me, please.
>
> **Ms. Ryan:** Rob, please copy this for me. Oh . . . and when is my appointment with Ms. Smith?

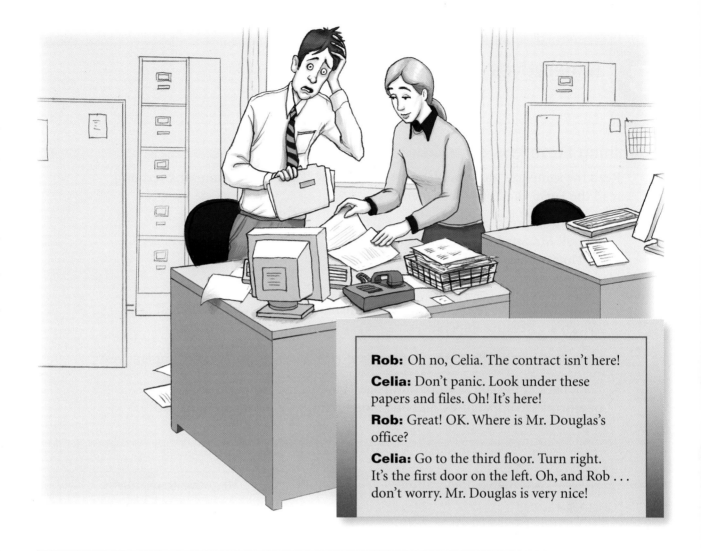

Rob: Oh no, Celia. The contract isn't here!

Celia: Don't panic. Look under these papers and files. Oh! It's here!

Rob: Great! OK. Where is Mr. Douglas's office?

Celia: Go to the third floor. Turn right. It's the first door on the left. Oh, and Rob . . . don't worry. Mr. Douglas is very nice!

---

contract: a legal paper
file: a collection of papers in a folder
immediately: right away; now

mailroom: a place in an office where people send letters and packages
panic: to feel fear and worry

A3 After You Read

Check (✓) the tasks that people ask Rob to do.

✓ **1.** take a package to the mailroom

___ **2.** make coffee

___ **3.** get lunch

___ **4.** make copies

___ **5.** write contracts

___ **6.** make phone calls

___ **7.** check appointments

___ **8.** file papers

B Imperatives

Examining Form

Read the sentences and complete the tasks below. Then discuss your answers and read the Form charts to check them.

 a. Do not forget.
 b. Call Mr. Snyder for me, please.
 c. Don't panic.
 d. Turn right.

1. The sentences above are imperatives. Which are affirmative imperatives? Which are negative imperatives?

2. How do we form affirmative imperatives? How do we form negative imperatives?

3. Look back at the conversations on pages 44–45. Find two more examples of affirmative imperatives, and one more example of a negative imperative.

Affirmative Imperatives	
BASE FORM OF VERB	
Take	the contract to Mr. Douglas.
Copy	this for me.
Call	the bank.

Negative Imperatives	
DO + NOT	**BASE FORM OF VERB**
Do not **Don't**	**worry.**
	smoke.
	forget.

- The subject of an imperative sentence is *you* (singular or plural), but we do not usually say or write the subject of the verb.
- Affirmative imperatives have only one form: the base form of the verb.
- Negative imperatives have two forms: *do not* + base form of verb and *don't* + base form of verb. We generally use *don't* + base form of verb in spoken English.

Listen to each sentence. Do you hear an affirmative or a negative imperative? Check (✓) the correct column.

	AFFIRMATIVE	NEGATIVE
1.		✓
2.		
3.		
4.		
5.		
6.		
7.		
8.		
9.		
10.		

A. Complete the sentences with affirmative imperatives. Use the verbs below.

go   open   repeat   take out
listen   read   sit   talk

1. _Repeat_ the directions.

2. _____ to your partner.

3. _____ a pencil.

4. _____ to your partner's instructions.

5. _____ Chapter 4.

6. _____ the door.

7. _____ on the couch.

8. _____ home.

B. Change the affirmative imperatives in part A into negative imperatives.

Don't repeat the directions.

A. Write office rules with affirmative and negative imperatives. Use the words and phrases. Punctuate your sentences correctly.

1. play/loud music _Don't play loud music._

2. be/friendly to clients _____

3. call/your friends _____

4. be/polite _____

5. arrive/on time _____

6. lose/important files _____

7. be/messy _____

8. help/your co-workers _____

9. do/your work _____

10. forget/meetings _____

B. Work with a partner. Take turns saying the sentences in part A.

Don't play loud music.

Imperatives

Examining Meaning and Use

Read the sentences and answer the questions below. Then discuss your answers and read the Meaning and Use Notes to check them.

a. Turn right at Grand Avenue.
b. Mix the sugar with the flour.
c. Watch out! The stove is hot.
d. Give me the book.

Which sentence gives:

_____ a command to do something?   _____ instructions about how to do something?

_____ a warning of danger?   _____ directions to a place?

Meaning and Use Notes

Common Uses of Imperatives

1A Use affirmative and negative imperatives to give commands, warnings, instructions, or directions.

1B Commands express the authority of one person over another. Commands usually express strong feelings.

Parent to Children	*Boss to Employees*	*Teacher to Student*
Sit down and **be** quiet!	**Be** on time for the meeting.	**Don't run** in the hallways.

1C Warnings express danger.

Bus Driver to Passenger	*Two Strangers on the Street*
Be careful! The steps are wet.	**Look out**! A truck!

1D Instructions give information about what to do. Instructions are more neutral than commands and warnings.

On a Test	*On a Copy Machine*
Underline the negative sentences.	**Deposit** quarters.

(Continued on page 50)

1E Directions are also neutral. Directions give information about how to go somewhere.

Turn right at the corner. The school is on the left.
Take Interstate 91 to Exit 3.

Polite Imperatives

2 *Please* makes an imperative more polite. We use *please* in commands and instructions. We do not use *please* in warnings and directions. *Please* comes at the beginning or at the end of an imperative sentence. Use a comma if *please* comes at the end.

Command	*Instruction*
Please sit down and **be** quiet!	**Write** your name on your paper, **please**.

Using *You* in Imperatives

3 Sometimes we use *you* at the beginning of an imperative sentence for emphasis or to talk to a specific person in a group we are talking to. You can also add the person's name.

Looking for Lost Car Keys
You look next to the sofa.
Gina, you look under the desk.

C1 Listening for Meaning and Use
▶ Notes 1A–3

🎧 Listen to each sentence. Choose the correct use of the imperative.

1. (instruction)   warning
2. warning   direction
3. command   instruction
4. warning   direction

5. instruction   command
6. command   warning
7. instruction   direction
8. direction   command

A. Read the commands and the situations. Match each situation to the appropriate command. In some cases, more than one answer may be possible.

Commands

  g   **1.** Keep the change.

_____ **2.** Follow me, please.

_____ **3.** Jack, you clean your room.

_____ **4.** Don't be late.

_____ **5.** Please be quiet.

_____ **6.** Do your homework.

_____ **7.** Do not park here.

_____ **8.** Show me your passport.

Situations

a. police officer to driver

b. teacher to students

c. customs officer to tourist

d. librarian to students

e. tour guide to tourists

f. boss to employee

g. customer to taxi driver

h. father to son

B. Choose five of the situations from part A. Write a different command for each situation. Use *please* to make the commands more polite. Punctuate your sentences correctly.

1. **Situation:** _customer to taxi driver_

    Command: _Turn right at the next corner, please._

2. **Situation:** _____

    Command: _____

3. **Situation:** _____

    Command: _____

4. **Situation:** _____

    Command: _____

5. **Situation:** _____

    Command: _____

6. **Situation:** _____

    Command: _____

Write an affirmative or negative imperative for each sign. Use the verbs below.

fasten   smoke   swim   take   turn   walk

1.

Fasten your seat belts.

3.

5.

2.

4.

6.

Vocabulary Notes

Prepositions of Location

Prepositions of location tell where someone or something is.

B is **on** the right.　　B is **behind** A.　　A is **next to** B.
B is **next to** A.

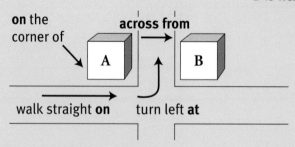

A is **on** the corner of High Street and Sherman Avenue.　　A is **across from** B.
Walk straight **on** High Street.　　Turn left **at** Sherman Avenue.

Look at the map. Complete each conversation with a preposition from the Vocabulary Notes. More than one preposition may be possible.

1. **A:** Is the school far?

    B: No, it' s not. Walk straight ___on___ Grand Street.
    ₁

2. **A:** Where is the bookstore?

    B: It's _____ the corner of Cherry Street and Main Street, _____
    ₁ ₂
    the hospital.

3. **A:** Is the gas station on Cherry Street?

    B: No, it isn't. It's _____ Grand Street, _____ the school.
    ₁ ₂

4. **A:** Where is the playground?

    B: Walk straight _____ Grand Street. It's _____ the school.
    ₁ ₂

5. **A:** Where is the supermarket? Is it far?

    B: Yes, it is. Walk straight _____ Grand Street. Turn right _____
    ₁ ₂
    Cherry Street. Walk straight _____ Cherry Street. Turn right
    ₃
    _____ Main Street. It's _____ coffee shop.
    ₄ ₅

C5 ▎**Identifying Imperatives** ▎► Note 1D

Read the instruction lines in this chapter. Find the imperative sentences. Write eight imperative sentences in your notebook. Compare your answers with a partner.

Discuss these questions.

C6 ▎**Writing Instructions** ▎► Note 1D

A. Complete the recipe for oatmeal. Use the verbs below to complete each instruction.

   add   boil   cook   lower   put   serve

1. _Put_____ one cup of water into a pan.

3. _____ half a cup of oatmeal.

5. _____ for five minutes.

2. _____ the water.

4. _____ the heat.

6. _____ with butter, milk, and sugar.

B. Write instructions on how to do something. For example, how to cook rice, polish your shoes, or hang a picture.

Boil two cups of water.
Add one cup of rice. . . .

Combining Form, Meaning, and Use

D1 Thinking About Meaning and Use

Complete each conversation. Then discuss your answers in small groups.

1. **A:** It's hot.

   B: _____
   - **a.** Open the window.
   - **b.** Put on a sweater.

2. **A:** The door is open.

   B: _____
   - **a.** Open it.
   - **b.** Close it.

3. **A:** It's Ana's birthday.

   B: _____
   - **a.** Don't be polite.
   - **b.** Buy her a present.

4. **A:** Is Jackie sick?

   B: Yes, she is. _____
   - **a.** Take her to the dance.
   - **b.** Please don't bother her.

5. **A:** It's dark in here.

   B: _____
   - **a.** Turn on the lights, please.
   - **b.** Don't turn off the lights.

6. **A:** Please don't sit on the table.

   B: _____
   - **a.** Oh, I'm sorry!
   - **b.** The chairs are comfortable.

7. **A:** The food is very hot!

   B: _____
   - **a.** Drink some water.
   - **b.** Put it in the oven.

8. **A:** It's sunny today.

   B: _____
   - **a.** Don't take your sunglasses.
   - **b.** Don't forget your sunglasses.

9. **A:** I'm late for work!

   B: _____
   - **a.** Take a taxi. Don't walk.
   - **b.** Walk. Don't take a taxi.

10. **A:** The mail is here.

    B: _____
    - **a.** Please get it.
    - **b.** Please send it.

Some of these sentences have errors. Find the errors and correct them.

1. ~~Not~~ Don't be noisy.

2. Brings a jacket.

3. Not go to the party.

4. Study tonight.

5. Be take a map.

6. No wear nice clothes.

7. Don't goes out.

8. Don't put the papers on the desk.

▶ Beyond the Classroom

Searching for Authentic Examples

Look for three imperatives on signs. Write them in your notebook and share them with your class. Copy the signs and exchange them with a partner. Compare your signs and imperatives with a partner.

Writing

Imagine that a friend is staying at your house while you are away. Follow the steps below to write a one-paragraph note to your friend.

1. Use these questions to make notes.
   - Does your friend need to feed your pets?
   - Does he or she need to water your plants?
   - Where do you keep the sheets and towels? Where are the keys?
   - Is there anything you want your friend to do or not to do?

2. Write a first draft. Use affirmative and negative imperatives.

3. Read your work carefully and circle grammar, spelling, and punctuation errors. Work with a partner to decide how to fix the errors and improve the content.

4. Rewrite your draft.

   Dear Carl,

   Welcome to my apartment. Please don't forget to feed my dog. Remember to change his water every day. The dog food is in the kitchen. . . .

Nouns

Introduction to Nouns

A A Nice Place to Live

A1 Before You Read

Discuss these questions.

Do you live in a house or an apartment? Do you like your neighborhood?

A2 Read

Read these advertisements. What do they advertise?

Apartments for Rent

Two apartments in a good neighborhood, each with:

- a living room
- 2 bedrooms
- 1 1/2 bathrooms
- a large kitchen
- a garage
- a swimming pool
- a laundry room

- an elevator
- no pets

RENT
$750
per month
utilities included

Call Alan Marshall: 978-555-0921

Studio Apartments in Beautiful Downtown Danvers

Lovely studios in an old home on Grand Street

In each apartment: a kitchenette, a bathroom, and a balcony (great for plants!).

No smokers, please.

Call Larry Clark, manager: 978-555-5010

The Perfect House for a Family

- 2 bathrooms
- 3 bedrooms
- an elegant living room
- a sunny dining room
- a new kitchen
- a garage
- near Glenview Elementary School
- rent: $1,500 per month

Available March 1

Call Thompson Realty Today:
978-555-3285

---

kitchenette: a very small kitchen in an apartment

rent: money that people pay for the use of a house or an apartment

studio (apartment): a small apartment with only one room and a bathroom

utilities: electricity, water, and gas for heating and cooking

A3 After You Read

Work with a partner. Find a place to live for each person or family. Choose from the three ads.

RENTERS	CHILDREN	INCOME PER MONTH	OTHER INFORMATION
Derek Dobson	none	$1,200	Derek is a student.
Sally and John Freeman	Alex, 10 Amy, 8 Kim, 4	$5,500	Sally and John are teachers.
Paul and Jenny Rivera	Chris, 17	$4,000	Chris is a swimmer.

B Singular Count Nouns

Examining Form

Read the sentences and complete the tasks below. Then discuss your answers and read the Form charts to check them.

a. Paul is an engineer.   **c.** Toronto is a city.
b. John is a teacher.   **d.** Choose an apartment.

1. Underline three names for people or places.

2. Circle the other singular nouns in each sentence.

3. Look for the words *a* or *an* in the sentences. When do we use *a*? When do we use *an*?

Singular Count Nouns		
	A/AN	**NOUN**
Amy is	a	**child.**
Pinehurst is		**town.**
Mark is	an	**electrician.**
Call		**ambulance.**

Overview

- Nouns are words we use for people, places, or things.
    swimmer   park   car
- Some nouns have singular and plural forms. We call these nouns *count nouns*. (See Chapter 5 for more information on count and noncount nouns.)
    one **swimmer**   two/three/four **swimmers**
- *A, an,* or *the* can come before a singular count noun.
- Use *a* before a singular count noun that begins with a consonant sound. Use *an* before a singular count noun that begins with a vowel sound.
- If a noun begins with a silent *h* (the *h* is not pronounced), use *an*. If the *h* is pronounced, use *a*.
    an hour   **a** house

- The letter *u* sometimes has a consonant sound. (We pronounce it like the *y* in *yellow*.) Use *a* when the initial *u* is pronounced *y*.

  a utility   **an** umbrella

Proper Nouns and Common Nouns

- Proper nouns are names of specific people, places, or things. Proper nouns begin with a capital letter.

  John   Grand Street   Miami

- All other nouns are common nouns.

⚠️ We do not usually use *a* or *an* before singular proper nouns.

B1) Listening for Form

🎧 Listen to each noun. Does it begin with a consonant sound or vowel sound? Check (✓) the correct column.

		CONSONANT SOUND	VOWEL SOUND
1.	hour		✓
2.	hospital		
3.	herb		
4.	hat		
5.	union		
6.	university		
7.	uncle		
8.	umpire		

B2) Identifying Nouns

A. Read the nouns. Write *P* for proper noun or *C* for common noun.

_P_ **1.** Toronto   ____ **4.** Julia Roberts

____ **2.** building   ____ **5.** book

____ **3.** Asia   ____ **6.** kitchen

B. Work with a partner. Write sentences with the nouns from part A. Use *a* or *an* with singular common nouns.

Toronto is my favorite city.

Complete the conversations with *a* or *an*. Write ✗ where it is not necessary to use *a* or *an*.

Conversation 1

Nesha: Is Soon-jun __a__ police officer?

　　　　　　　　　　　¹

Victor: No, he's __an__ ambulance driver.

　　　　　　　　²

Conversation 2

Sara: Is she _____ student?

　　　　　　　¹

Sam: No, she's _____ employee at the hospital. She's _____ receptionist.

　　　　　　　　　²　　　　　　　　　　　　　　　　　³

Conversation 3

Reiko: Are you in _____ dorm?

　　　　　　　　　¹

Marta: No, I am in _____ house near campus.

　　　　　　　　　²

Conversation 4

Celia: Where is _____ Yale University?

　　　　　　　　¹

Hanna: It's in _____ town in _____ Connecticut.

　　　　　　　²　　　　　　³

Conversation 5

Lee: What is _____ umpire?

　　　　　　　¹

Sam: _____ umpire is _____ baseball official.

　　　²　　　　　　³

Conversation 6

Chris: _____ apartment is for rent in my building.

　　　　¹

Stefan: Is it _____ studio?

　　　　　　　　²

Conversation 7

Jenny: Your neighborhood is _____ nice place to live.

　　　　　　　　　　　　　　¹

Lisa: Yes, and it's near _____ Lyle Park.

　　　　　　　　　　　　²

C Plural Count Nouns

Examining Form

Read the sentences and complete the tasks below. Then discuss your answers and read the Form charts to check them.

a. Sally and John are teachers.   **c.** Balconies are great for plants.

b. Amy and Kim are children.   **d.** People are friendly in San Diego.

1. Underline the plural nouns that end in *-s* or *-es*.

2. Plural nouns that do not end in *-s* or *-es* are irregular. Circle the two irregular plural nouns.

Plural Count Nouns	
	NOUN
We are	**swimmers.**
Amy and Kim are	**children.**
They are	**women.**
Where are the	**balconies?**

Overview

- Add *-s* or *-es* to the singular form of a regular count noun to make it plural. See Appendix 1 for spelling rules for plural nouns.

- Plural nouns that do not end in *-s* or *-es* are irregular. Some common irregular nouns are:

  SINGULAR — PLURAL

  child — children   woman — women   man — men   person — people

  tooth — teeth   foot — feet   mouse — mice

- See Appendix 1 for a list of irregular plural nouns.

- *The* or no article can come before plural nouns. Do not use *a* or *an* before plural nouns.

Proper Nouns

- Use *the* + a plural proper noun for the family name of two or more people.

  the Riveras   the Sanchezes   the Kims

C1 Listening for Form

Listen to each noun. Is it singular or plural? Check (✓) the correct column.

	SINGULAR	PLURAL
1.	✓	
2.		
3.		
4.		
5.		
6.		
7.		
8.		

C2 Spelling Regular Plural Nouns

Write the plural forms of these nouns. Use Appendix 1 for help.

1. dictionary   _dictionaries_

2. balcony   _____

3. bedroom   _____

4. radio   _____

5. boy   _____

6. garage   _____

7. potato   _____

8. brush   _____

C3 Working with Irregular Plural Nouns

Complete each sentence with the correct irregular plural form of the noun in parentheses.

1. The _children_ (child) are in the park.

2. Two hundred _____ (person) are in line for the new Tom Cruise movie!

3. The _____ (man) are in my class.

4. Your smile is beautiful. Your _____ (tooth) are very white.

5. The _____ (woman) are from my hometown.

6. I'm not a good dancer. My _____ (foot) are too big!

Pronunciation Notes

Pronunciation of Regular Plural Nouns

We pronounce the final sound of regular plural nouns in three different ways.

1. As /s/ after the voiceless sounds /p/, /t/, /k/, /f/, and /θ/.

   caps   apartments   packs   cliffs   months

2. As /ɪz/ after the sounds /dʒ/, /tʃ/, /s/, /z/, /ʃ/, /ʒ/, and /ks/.

   bridges   watches   classes   quizzes   dishes   garages   boxes

3. As /z/ after all other sounds.

   doctors   employees   kitchens   words   lives

C4   Pronouncing Regular Plural Nouns

A. 🎧 Listen to each plural noun. What ending do you hear? Check (✓) the correct column.

		/s/	/z/	/ɪz/
1.	cars		✓	
2.	pencils			
3.	wishes			
4.	roommates			
5.	nouns			
6.	maps			

B. Work with a partner. Take turns pronouncing the pairs of words below. Choose the correct sound for the plural ending.

1. road — roads   /s/   (/z/)   /ɪz/

2. clock — clocks   /s/   /z/   /ɪz/

3. sentence — sentences   /s/   /z/   /ɪz/

4. room — rooms   /s/   /z/   /ɪz/

5. belief — beliefs   /s/   /z/   /ɪz/

6. excuse — excuses   /s/   /z/   /ɪz/

7. garage — garages   /s/   /z/   /ɪz/

8. apartment — apartments   /s/   /z/   /ɪz/

The Functions of Nouns

Examining Meaning and Use

Read the sentences and answer the questions below. Then discuss your answers and read the Meaning and Use Notes to check them.

    a. Flowers are expensive.
    b. Roses are flowers.
    c. The library is next to the bank.
    d. Open the door.

1. Which sentences have nouns used as subjects? Which sentence does not?

2. Which sentence has a noun after a verb other than *be*?

3. Which sentence has a noun after *be*?

4. Which sentence has a noun after a preposition?

Meaning and Use Notes

Nouns As Subjects

1 We can use a noun (or pronoun) as the subject of a sentence. The subject of a sentence with *be* tells who or what the sentence is about.

    Barry King is the manager.
    Computers are useful.
    Teresa and **Pete** are children.

Nouns As Objects

2 We can use a noun as the object of a verb. The object usually receives the action of the verb.

    Call the **manager**.   Please make the **sandwiches** now.

Nouns After *Be*

3 We can use a noun after the verb *be*. We use this noun to define or describe the subject of the sentence.

A studio <u>is</u> a small **apartment**.   The Freemans <u>are</u> **teachers**.

Nouns After Prepositions

4 We can use a noun after a preposition. After many prepositions nouns refer to locations.

Mr. Clark is <u>on</u> the **telephone**.   The school is <u>in</u> **town**.
Medford is <u>near</u> the **city**.   Steve is <u>from</u> **Boston**.

D1) Listening for Meaning and Use   ▶ Notes 2, 3

Listen to the sentences. How do we use each noun? Check (✓) the correct column.

		RECEIVES THE ACTION	DESCRIBES THE SUBJECT
1.	vegetables	✓	
2.	building		
3.	apartments		
4.	newspaper		
5.	landlord		
6.	house		
7.	utilities		
8.	utensil		
9.	door		
10.	swimmer		

D2) Writing an Ad   ▶ Notes 1–4

Write an ad for a place to rent. The ad is for a college bulletin board. Is it a house or apartment? Describe it. Where is it? Who is the contact person?

Studio apartment for rent . . .

Read the messages. Then answer the questions.

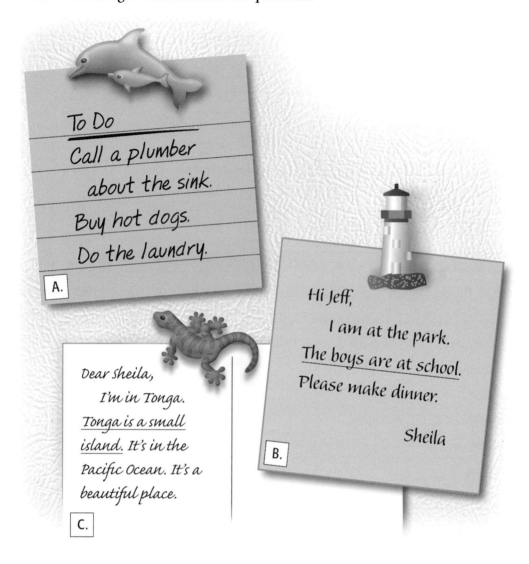

A.

To Do

Call a plumber
   about the sink.
Buy hot dogs.
Do the laundry.

B.

Hi Jeff,

   I am at the park.
The boys are at school.
Please make dinner.

               Sheila

C.

Dear Sheila,
   I'm in Tonga.
Tonga is a small
island. It's in the
Pacific Ocean. It's a
beautiful place.

1. Look at message A. Which three nouns receive the action of the verb?
   plumber, . . .

2. Look at the underlined sentence in message B. Which noun is the sentence about?

3. Look at the underlined sentence in message C. Which noun defines Tonga?

4. Find four examples of prepositions + nouns used for locations.

E Combining Form, Meaning, and Use

E1 Thinking About Meaning and Use

Complete each conversation. Then discuss your answers in small groups.

1. **A:** Call the children, please.

   B: Sure. _____
   - **a.** Where are they?
   - **b.** Where is she?

2. **A:** Is this apartment for rent?

   B: Yes. _____
   - **a.** It's available in June.
   - **b.** They are available in June.

3. **A:** When is the last day of classes?

   B: _____
   - **a.** They are in December.
   - **b.** It's in December.

4. **A:** Is your father a doctor?

   B: _____
   - **a.** No, teachers.
   - **b.** No, a teacher.

5. **A:** Is Albany near Los Angeles?

   B: No, _____
   - **a.** they aren't.
   - **b.** it isn't.

6. **A:** Where are the women?

   B: _____
   - **a.** They're at work.
   - **b.** She's at work.

E2 Editing

Some of these sentences have errors. Find the errors and correct them.

1. Dustin hoffman is a famous actor.

2. When is a Christmas?

3. The Watson are here.

4. The childs are happy.

5. They are employees at Microsoft.

6. Eat a apple every day.

7. Kenya is country in Africa.

8. Don't write in the books.

9. A Spain is a beautiful country.

10. The pen is in my bag.

11. Marta and Stefan are student in my class.

12. The books are on the shelves.

Beyond the Classroom

Searching for Authentic Examples

Look in an English-language newspaper or on the Internet for advertisements for apartments. Find three singular nouns and three plural nouns. Write them in your notebook and share them with your class.

Speaking

A scavenger hunt is a game for teams. Follow these steps to organize and participate in a scavenger hunt.

1. In teams, make a list of 15 objects for a scavenger hunt. Make the objects small or easy to bring to class.

2. Use *a/an* or a number before each noun in your list.

3. Exchange lists with another team. Find the objects from the list and bring them to class. The team with the most things on the list is the winner.

Scavenger Hunt List

an athletic shoe
an English dictionary
an earring
two pencils
a postcard from a different country . . .

Introduction to Count and Noncount Nouns

Protect Our Environment

A1 Before You Read

Discuss these questions.

Is the environment important to you? Is it important to protect the environment? Why?

A2 Read

Read the flyer from an environmental organization on the following page. What are some ways to protect the environment?

A3 After You Read

Match the first half of each sentence to the second half.

_e_ **1.** Turn off . . .   **a.** energy-efficient office machines.

____ **2.** Use . . .   **b.** paper and plastic.

____ **3.** Reuse . . .   **c.** the curtains.

____ **4.** Recycle . . .   **d.** old furniture.

____ **5.** Donate . . .   **e.** the lights.

____ **6.** Close . . .   **f.** the heat.

____ **7.** Wash . . .   **g.** glass bottles.

____ **8.** Lower . . .   **h.** clothes in cold water.

PROTECT OUR ENVIRONMENT

Here are tips for home and office:

CONSERVE ENERGY

At Home

- Turn off the lights.
- Use energy-efficient light bulbs.
- Use appliances efficiently. For example, wash clothes in cold water.
- Lower the heat.
- Close the curtains on hot days.

In the Office

- Turn off all equipment at night.
- Use energy-efficient photocopying machines, computers, and printers.

RECYCLE

At Home

- Recycle cans, glass, plastic, and newspapers.
- Reuse glass bottles.

In the Office

- Recycle paper.
- Donate old computers and equipment to schools.
- Donate old office furniture.

---

appliances: machines we use at home
conserve: not to waste
donate: to give something for free to an organization or group
energy-efficient: not using much energy

equipment: things that we need to perform a particular activity
protect: to keep safe
tips: pieces of useful advice

B Count and Noncount Nouns

Examining Form

Read the sentences and complete the task below. Then discuss your answers and read the Form charts to check them.

1a. The <u>bottle</u> is in the <u>garbage</u>.
1b. The <u>bottles</u> are in the <u>garbage</u>.
2a. Turn off the <u>computer</u>. Save <u>electricity</u>.
2b. Turn off the <u>computers</u>. Save <u>electricity</u>.

Look at the underlined nouns. Which nouns have both singular and plural forms? Which nouns have only one form?

Singular Count Nouns			
	NOUN	VERB	
A	**computer**	is	expensive.
The	**umbrella**		inexpensive.

Plural Count Nouns			
	NOUN	VERB	
	Computers	are	expensive.
The	**umbrellas**		inexpensive.

Noncount Nouns			
	NOUN	VERB	
	Pollution	is	unhealthy.
The	**air**		clean.

Count Nouns

- We use count nouns for people, places, or things we can count. Count nouns usually have singular and plural forms.
- Some count nouns have only a plural form.
  The **jeans** are dirty.   The **clothes** are new.   The **sunglasses** are on the table.
- Some count nouns have the same singular and plural form.
  one **fish**   three **fish**   one **sheep**   two **sheep**
- Singular count nouns occur with *a/an* or *the*. Plural count nouns occur with *the* or no article.

B1 Listening for Form

🎧 Listen to each sentence. Is the noun count or noncount? Check (✓) the correct column.

	COUNT NOUN	NONCOUNT NOUN
1.	✓	
2.		
3.		
4.		
5.		
6.		

B2 Identifying Count and Noncount Nouns

Work with a partner. Underline the nouns in each sentence. Write *C* for count or *NC* for noncount above each noun.

        NC   C

1. Transportation is expensive in a big city.

2. Pollution is not a problem in my country.

3. Buy a bicycle. Reduce pollution.

4. Close the curtains, please. The room is hot.

5. You are the last person in the office. Turn off the equipment, please.

6. Please don't put newspapers in the garbage. Recycle them.

Form sentences with count and noncount nouns. Use the words and phrases. Make all necessary changes. Punctuate your sentences correctly.

1. The environment/be/important

   <u>The environment is important.</u>

2. Energy/not/be/cheap

   _____

3. The computers/not/be/on

   _____

4. The refrigerator door/be/open

   _____

5. Our air conditioner/be/not/energy efficient

   _____

6. New furniture/be/expensive

   _____

Complete the advertisement with *is* or *are*.

<u>Are</u> clean clothes important to you? Then
₁
use Oxybright! Wash your clothes with Oxybright!

Oxybright _____ a powerful detergent. Dirt on
₂
your jeans? Don't worry. Dirty jeans _____
₃
not a problem with Oxybright. _____ your
₄
windows dirty? Use Oxybright! That's right. This

amazing product _____ a detergent and a
₅
cleaner! _____ Oxybright expensive? Great news!
₆
It's only $5.99!

**BUY OXYBRIGHT!
IT'S ONLY $5.99!**

OXYBRIGHT

Count and Noncount Nouns

Examining Meaning and Use

Read the sentences and answer the questions below. Then discuss your answers and read the Meaning and Use Notes to check them.

1a. Oh no! A gray hair!
1b. Long hair is beautiful.

2a. Chocolate is delicious.
2b. The chocolates are from Jim.

1. Underline the noncount nouns and circle the count nouns in each pair of sentences.

2. Which sentences are about individual items? Which are more general statements about a category or a kind of thing?

Meaning and Use Notes

Count Nouns vs. Noncount Nouns

1A Count nouns are people, places, or things that we can count as individual items. Noncount nouns are things we cannot count or think about as individual items.

1B Count and noncount nouns are sometimes related in meaning. Noncount nouns sometimes refer to a class of objects. Count nouns refer to a particular example of something. Compare the nouns in the two columns. See Appendix 2 for a list of common noncount nouns.

Count Nouns	Noncount Nouns
an apple	fruit
a job	work
a trip	travel
a dollar bill	money
a suitcase	luggage
a necklace	jewelry

(Continued on page 80)

2A Many noncount nouns are substances and materials. See Appendix 2 for a list of common noncount nouns.

Solids	*Gases*	*Materials*
chalk, glass	oxygen, air	wood, plastic

Liquids	*Grains and Powders*
shampoo, water	sugar, flour

2B Noncount nouns also refer to feelings and ideas, school subjects, and activities.

Feelings and Ideas	*School Subjects*	*Activities*
love, knowledge	biology, mathematics	basketball, swimming

General vs. Individual

3 Some nouns are both count and noncount. However, their meanings are different. Count nouns refer to individual things. Noncount nouns are usually more general.

Count (Individual)	*Noncount (General)*
Two large **coffees**, please. (two cups of coffee)	Don't drink **coffee**. (the drink)
Give me the **basketball**. (the ball)	**Basketball** is exciting. (the sport)
A **lamb** is a young sheep. (the animal)	**Lamb** is good in stew. (the meat)
Hand in your **paper**. (a piece of paper)	Recycle **paper**. (the material)

C1 Listening for Meaning and Use ▶ Notes 1A–3

🎧 Listen to each sentence and look at the noun. Does the speaker use it as a count noun or a noncount noun? Check (✓) the correct column.

		COUNT	NONCOUNT
1.	education		✓
2.	coffee		
3.	glass		
4.	chocolate		
5.	glass		
6.	hair		
7.	basketball		
8.	paper		

Describing Classroom Objects ► Notes 1A–2A

Find six objects in your classroom. What material are they made of? Write the name of the object and the material in your notebook. Label the nouns count or noncount.

desk = count
wood = noncount

C3 **Thinking About Count and Noncount Nouns** ► Notes 1A, 2A, 2B

A. Write the nouns in the correct categories below.

books	cars	feet	jewelry	pencil	teeth
boxes	children	flowers	mathematics	people	telephone
bracelet	computers	furniture	mice	radios	weather
building	equipment	jacket	music	sofa	women

COUNT NOUNS

SINGULAR   PLURAL

     Regular   Irregular

bracelet   books   children

_____   _____   _____

_____   _____   _____

_____   _____   _____

_____   _____   _____

_____   _____   _____

NONCOUNT NOUNS

equipment

_____

_____

_____

_____

B. Choose four count nouns and four noncount nouns from the list in part A. Use each word in a sentence.

Don't buy the expensive bracelet.

A. Read each pair of sentences. One sentence uses the count form of a noun. The other uses the noncount form of the same noun. Is the underlined noun used as a count noun or a noncount noun? Write *C* for count noun or *N* for noncount noun.

1. __C__ **a.** A <u>baseball</u> is round and white.

   __N__ **b.** <u>Baseball</u> is a popular sport in Japan.

2. _____ **a.** Recycle <u>glass</u>.

   _____ **b.** Give me a <u>glass</u>, please.

3. _____ **a.** <u>Business</u> is slow now. The economy is bad.

   _____ **b.** Don't start a <u>business</u>! Go to college.

4. _____ **a.** Don't make a <u>change</u> in your life now.

   _____ **b.** Give me <u>change</u> for the telephone, please

5. _____ **a.** Eat more <u>fish</u>. It is good for your health.

   _____ **b.** Three <u>fish</u> are in the aquarium.

6. _____ **a.** A good <u>education</u> is expensive in the United States.

   _____ **b.** <u>Education</u> is important.

B. Each noun below has a count and a noncount meaning. Write one sentence using the count form of the noun and one sentence using the noncount form. Use a dictionary if you need help.

1. hair

   Waiter, there's a hair in my soup.
   Her hair is red.

2. glass

3. chicken

4. football

5. coffee

6. cake

Customer: *Waiter, there is a hair in my soup.*
Waiter: *Don't worry, sir. It's free.*

D Combining Form, Meaning, and Use

D1 Thinking About Meaning and Use

Complete each conversation. Then discuss your answers in small groups.

1. **A:** Wash the clothes.

   B: _____
   - **(a.)** OK. Where are they?
   - **b.** Sure. Where is it?

2. **A:** Where's the meat?

   B: _____
   - **a.** It's on the table.
   - **b.** They're in the refrigerator.

3. **A:** Is this plastic?

   B: No, _____
   - **a.** it's a glass.
   - **b.** it's glass.

4. **A:** Get me a coffee, please.

   B: _____
   - **a.** One pound or two?
   - **b.** With cream or sugar?

5. **A:** What is your favorite sport?

   B: _____
   - **a.** A football.
   - **b.** Football.

6. **A:** Buy your mother a present for her birthday.

   B: Okay. Is _____ a good gift?
   - **a.** earrings
   - **b.** jewelry

D2 Editing

Some of these sentences have errors. Find the errors and correct them.

1. Don't drink the ~~waters~~. *water*

2. Comb your hairs.

3. Your new clothes are beautiful.

4. Mathematics are easy.

5. The money is in the bank.

6. The furniture are new.

7. A football is an exciting sport.

8. Give me a coffee, please.

Beyond the Classroom

Searching for Authentic Examples

Collect English-language take-out restaurant menus or look for them on the Internet. Find five count nouns and five noncount nouns. Write them in your notebook. Share the menus and your findings with your class.

Speaking

Think about your school or your job. Make a list of at least ten nouns that you use when you talk about your school or job. Use a dictionary if you need help. Then show your list to a partner.

My job: groceries, manager, cash register . . .

Choose five words from your list and make a sentence for each to explain its importance. Make sure you use the noun correctly as a singular or plural count noun or as a noncount noun.

Groceries are expensive at my supermarket.

Adjectives and Pronouns

Descriptive Adjectives

Westbrook College News

A1 Before You Read

Discuss these questions.

What are classified advertisements? Does your college newspaper have classified advertisements? What do people advertise?

A2 Read

Read these classified ads from an on-line college newspaper. What do students at Westbrook College advertise?

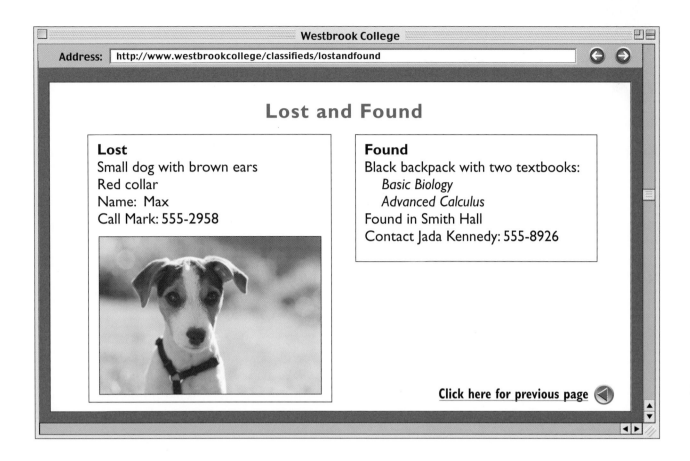

Lost and Found

Lost
Small dog with brown ears
Red collar
Name: Max
Call Mark: 555-2958

Found
Black backpack with two textbooks:
  Basic Biology
  Advanced Calculus
Found in Smith Hall
Contact Jada Kennedy: 555-8926

Click here for previous page

---

collar: a band around the neck of a dog or cat
condition: how well something works; how it looks

pet: an animal that you keep in your home
wool: material from sheep's hair used to make clothes

A3 After You Read

Check (✓) the things in the classified ads.

_✓_ **1.** a lost dog

____ **2.** CDs from the '80s and '90s

____ **3.** a diamond ring

____ **4.** a student desk

____ **5.** a new dress

____ **6.** a black backpack

B Descriptive Adjectives

Examining Form

Complete the tasks below. Then discuss your answers and read the Form charts to check them.

1. Adjectives describe nouns. Underline the nouns in the phrases below. Circle the adjectives.

    large pets   red collar   serious student   nice apartment

2. Look at the sentences below. Underline the nouns and circle the adjectives in each sentence. Which nouns are singular? Which nouns are plural? Does the form of the adjective change with singular and plural nouns?

    a. It is a small dog with a red collar.

    b. They are small dogs with red collars.

3. Look back at the ads on pages 88–89. Find four more adjectives. What nouns do they describe?

Adjectives After *Be*		
	NOUN	BE	ADJECTIVE
The	dog	is	**black.**
	dogs	are	

Adjectives Before Nouns			
	ADJECTIVE	NOUN	
The	**new**	teacher	is here.
They are	**friendly**	students.	

Overview
- Adjectives describe nouns.
- Adjectives have only one form. Use the same adjective with singular and plural nouns.
    a **friendly** student   **friendly** students

Adjectives After *Be*
- An adjective can occur alone after *be*. When two adjectives come after *be*, separate them with *and*.
    The apartment is bright **and** quiet.
- ⚠ Do not use *a, an,* or *the* with adjectives that occur alone after *be*.
    *The dog is a black. (INCORRECT)

Adjectives Before Nouns
- An adjective can come before a noun.

- When an adjective comes before a singular noun, use *a* before the adjective if it begins with a consonant sound. Use *an* before the adjective if it begins with a vowel sound.

  <u>a</u> **new** apartment   <u>an</u> **old** apartment

- Some nouns can function as adjectives when they describe other nouns.

  a **wedding** dress   a **leather** collar

B1 Listening for Form

🎧 Listen to the sentences. Do the sentences have adjectives or not? Check (✓) the correct column.

	ADJECTIVE	NO ADJECTIVE
1.	✓	
2.		
3.		
4.		
5.		
6.		
7.		
8.		

B2 Identifying Adjectives

Circle the adjectives in the sentences. Then draw an arrow to show the noun they describe.

1. The tea is (hot.)

2. The oatmeal cookies are delicious.

3. The students are intelligent.

4. Amsterdam is a pretty city.

5. The weather is cloudy and rainy.

6. He is a strong athlete.

7. Chocolate cake is on the menu.

8. We are tired and hungry.

A. Form sentences with adjectives. Use the words. Punctuate your sentences correctly.

1. drive/don't/an/car/old

   Don't drive an old car.

2. is/an/he/student/excellent

   _____

3. new/dress/buy/a

   _____

4. famous/a/writer/Hiro/is

   _____

5. is/small/a/apartment/it

   _____

6. ink/red/use/don't

   _____

B. Add the word in parentheses to each sentence. Write your sentences in your notebook. Make any necessary changes.

1. Jack Nicholson is an actor. (famous)

   Jack Nicholson is a famous actor.

2. Don't buy a car. (expensive)

3. Send them an invitation. (wedding)

4. Tell us a story. (interesting)

5. She's a student. (university)

6. It's a mistake. (unusual)

Descriptions with Adjectives

Examining Meaning and Use

Read the sentences and complete the tasks below. Then discuss your answers and read the Meaning and Use Notes to check them.

a. His hair is red.
b. He is Korean.
c. She is a young woman.

d. The book is interesting.
e. The building is small.
f. The tables are round.

1. Underline the adjectives.

2. Write the adjectives next to the correct categories below.

quality/opinion: _____   age: _____   origin: _____

size: _____   color: _____   shape: _____

Meaning and Use Notes

> ### Categories of Adjectives
>
> **1A** Adjectives describe nouns in many ways.
>
> | | |
> |---|---|
> | *Quality/Opinion:* It's a **nice** ring. | *Color:* My **brown** belt is lost. |
> | *Size:* Where's the **little** dog? | *Origin:* My aunt is **Brazilian**. |
> | *Age:* It's an **old** dress. | *Shape:* The table is **round**. |
>
> **1B** Below are some common adjectives. See Appendix 9 for a list of common adjectives by categories.
>
> | Quality/ Opinion | Size | Age | Color | Origin | Shape |
> |---|---|---|---|---|---|
> | beautiful | big | new | blue | Chinese | oval |
> | expensive | large | old | brown | European | round |
> | happy | little | young | green | French | square |
> | hard | short | | red | Italian | |
> | ugly | small | | white | Japanese | |

(Continued on page 94)

> **Using Nouns as Adjectives**
>
> **2** We often use a noun to describe another noun. In this case, the first noun always describes the second noun.
>
> a **table** lamp = a lamp that you put on a table   a **wool** hat = a hat made of wool
> a **wedding** dress = a dress for a wedding   a **winter** coat = a coat for winter

---

C1 Listening for Meaning and Use

► Notes 1A, 1B

Listen to these sentences about a restaurant. Choose the correct answer.

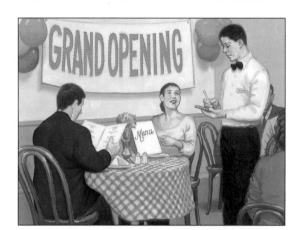

1. a. Tony's isn't new.
   (b.) Tony's isn't old.

2. a. The owner is famous.
   b. The restaurant is famous.

3. a. The chef is from Italy.
   b. The chef is in Italy.

4. a. The chef is good.
   b. The chef isn't good.

5. a. It's a cheap restaurant.
   b. It's an expensive restaurant.

6. a. The food at Tony's is good.
   b. The food at Tony's isn't good.

C2 Asking About Qualities and Opinions

► Notes 1A, 1B

Work with a partner. Think about your school. Take turns asking and answering questions about these topics. Use adjectives of quality or opinion. See Appendix 9 for a list of common adjectives.

1. cafeteria food

> A: *How is the cafeteria food?*
> B: *It's terrible.*
> OR
> A: *What is the cafeteria food like?*
> B: *It's great.*

2. library

3. teachers

4. sports teams

5. students

6. computer lab

A. Put each adjective into the correct category in the chart.

beautiful	large	old	red	small	tall
Brazilian	new	orange	round	Spanish	yellow
Italian	noisy	oval	slow	square	young

QUALITY/OPINION	SIZE	AGE	COLOR	ORIGIN	SHAPE
beautiful					

B. Write six sentences in your notebook. Use some of the adjectives from the chart in part A.

Nepal is a beautiful country.

C4 **Understanding Nouns as Adjectives** ► Note 2

A. Complete the definitions with the correct words.

1. An airport bus is a kind of ((bus)/ airport).

2. A ticket office is a kind of (office / ticket).

3. Milk chocolate is a kind of (milk / chocolate).

4. Chocolate milk is a kind of (milk / chocolate).

5. A pocket calculator is a kind of (calculator / pocket)

6. A car seat is a kind of (car / seat)

B. Complete the definitions. Use nouns as adjectives.

1. A _school library_ is a library in a school.

2. A _____ is an earring made of gold.

3. A _____ is a ticket for a theater.

4. A _____ is a plate made of paper.

5. A _____ is a student at a university.

6. A _____ is a cup used for coffee.

A. These ads are from a college bulletin board. Complete each one. Use some of the adjectives below. More than one answer may be possible.

A __small__ cat with a _____ collar. His eyes are _____. Name: Max

Call Naomi: 555-3366

1. white, grey, large, small

A _____ apartment with two _____ bedrooms for _____ students.

Call 555-4291. Ask for Kim.

2. bright, cheap, quiet, big

Furniture for Sale

_____ sofa
_____ table
_____ chairs
_____ prices

Call 555-4545

3. antique, European, low, new

Call Gloria: 555-9292

A _____ sweater with _____ buttons and _____ sleeves.

4. long, round, yellow, green

B. Show your advertisements to a partner. How are they different?

C. In your notebook write a three-line ad about a lost object. Use adjectives or nouns as adjectives to describe the object.

Lost: a baseball hat . . .

D Combining Form, Meaning, and Use

D1 Thinking About Meaning and Use

Complete each conversation. Then discuss your answers in small groups.

1. **A:** What's your apartment like?

   B: _____

      a. I'm glad.

      ⓑ It's small.

2. **A:** How's your homework?

   B: _____

      a. It's hard.

      b. It's pretty.

3. **A:** Who's that?

   B: _____

      a. A student newspaper.

      b. A new student.

4. **A:** Where is your brother?

   B: On the _____

      a. school bus.

      b. bus schedule.

5. **A:** Is your school large?

   B: No, it's _____

      a. small

      b. old

6. **A:** Twenty people for dinner! Think about all the dirty dishes!

   B: _____

      a. Try expensive dishes.

      b. Try paper plates.

D2 Editing

Some of these sentences have errors. Find the errors and correct them.

1. She's ~~a~~ tall.

2. Baseball is a fantastic game.

3. Buy me a expensive ring.

4. His roommate is smart and handsome.

5. The girl short is my friend.

6. Eva and Amy are great runners.

7. Bring the bigs books.

8. Buy him a sweater wool.

▶ Beyond the Classroom

Searching for Authentic Examples

Look for ads in an English-language newspaper or on the Internet. Find five adjectives that are new to you. Find their meanings in the dictionary. Write the meanings in your notebook and share them with your class. What noun does each adjective describe?

Writing

Imagine you want to sell some things in your house or apartment. Follow the steps below to write an ad for a bulletin board.

1. Use these notes to plan your writing.
   - Make a list of the objects for sale.
   - Think of some adjectives to describe the objects.
   - Remember to include the name of a contact person and a phone number.

2. Write your draft. Use a variety of adjectives.

3. Read your work carefully and circle grammar, spelling, and punctuation errors. Work with a partner to decide how to fix the errors and improve the content.

4. Rewrite your draft. Draw pictures or add photographs to your ad. Put the advertisement on the wall of your classroom.

MOVING SALE

classical CDs   small table

jazz records   old hats

rare books   ...and much more!

Call Andrew: 555-0002

Possessives and Demonstratives

A Keeping in Touch

A1 Before You Read

Discuss these questions.

How do you communicate with your friends? Do you e-mail? Do you write letters? Which do you prefer?

A2 Read

Read these e-mail messages. How is Koji's life different from Alan's?

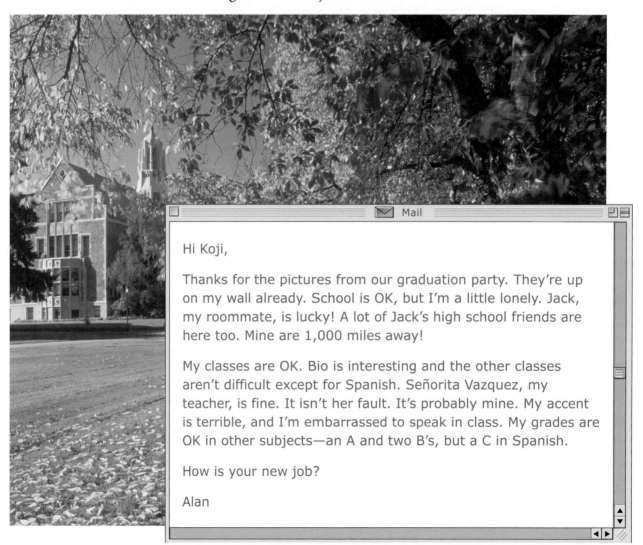

Hi Koji,

Thanks for the pictures from our graduation party. They're up on my wall already. School is OK, but I'm a little lonely. Jack, my roommate, is lucky! A lot of Jack's high school friends are here too. Mine are 1,000 miles away!

My classes are OK. Bio is interesting and the other classes aren't difficult except for Spanish. Señorita Vazquez, my teacher, is fine. It isn't her fault. It's probably mine. My accent is terrible, and I'm embarrassed to speak in class. My grades are OK in other subjects—an A and two B's, but a C in Spanish.

How is your new job?

Alan

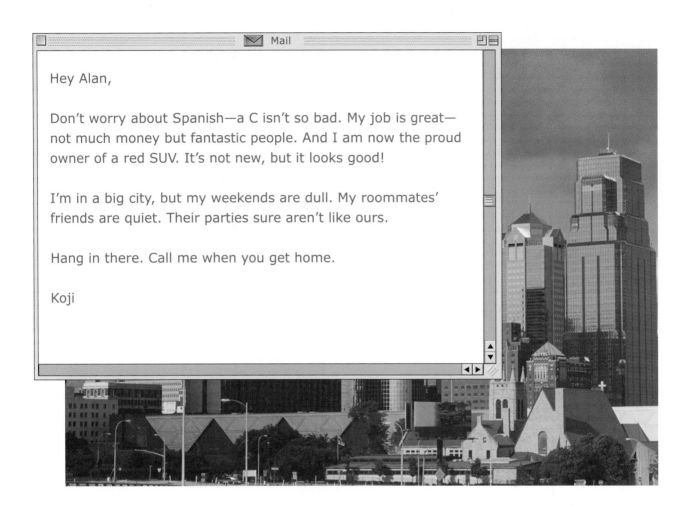

Hey Alan,

Don't worry about Spanish—a C isn't so bad. My job is great—not much money but fantastic people. And I am now the proud owner of a red SUV. It's not new, but it looks good!

I'm in a big city, but my weekends are dull. My roommates' friends are quiet. Their parties sure aren't like ours.

Hang in there. Call me when you get home.

Koji

Bio: abbreviation for Biology
embarrassed: uncomfortable or ashamed
fault: responsibility for a mistake

hang in there: be patient
subjects: areas of study, e.g., math, history
SUV (sport utility vehicle): a large vehicle similar to a van

A3 After You Read

Write *T* for true or *F* for false for each statement.

__T__ **1.** Alan is lonely.

_____ **2.** Jack is Alan's roommate.

_____ **3.** Spanish is hard for Alan.

_____ **4.** Koji doesn't like his new job.

_____ **5.** Koji enjoys his weekends.

_____ **6.** Koji has a red SUV.

B Possessive Nouns, Possessive Adjectives, and *Whose*

Examining Form

Read the sentences and complete the tasks below. Then discuss your answers and read the Form charts to check them.

1a. My <u>roommate's</u> friends are quiet. He's noisy.
1b. My <u>roommates'</u> friends are quiet. They're noisy.

2a. My brother is tall. I'm short.
2b. Their brother is tall. They are short.

1. Look at sentences 1a and 1b. Look at the underlined possessive nouns. Which noun is singular? Which is plural? How do you know?

2. Look at sentences 2a and 2b. Possessive adjectives come directly before nouns. Underline the nouns. Circle the possessive adjectives.

POSSESSIVE NOUNS

Singular		
NOUN + 'S		
Karen's	friend	is nice.
My sister's		

Plural			
	REGULAR NOUN + '		
The	**students'**	classroom	is small.
	teachers'	classrooms	are small.
	IRREGULAR NOUN + 'S		
The	**women's**	apartment	is bright and sunny.
	children's	classes	are interesting.

- Use an apostrophe + -s ('s) after singular nouns to form the possessive.
- For singular nouns that end in -s, add an apostrophe alone or 's. Either one is correct.
  Marcus' roommate   Marcus**'s** roommate
- For regular plural nouns, add an apostrophe alone to form the possessive.
- For irregular plural nouns, add 's.
- For two or more nouns together, add 's to the last noun.
  Dan and Karen**'s** mother
- Possessive nouns usually come before another noun.

- Possessive nouns can occur alone if the reference to a noun is clear.

    Is she the boy's mother or the girl's (mother)?

⚠ In informal writing, we sometimes see contractions with a noun + *is*. Do not confuse a possessive *'s* with a contraction.

    John's last name is Vazquez.   "John's here." (John is here.)

POSSESSIVE ADJECTIVES AND *WHOSE*

	Possessive Adjectives	
SUBJECT PRONOUN	POSSESSIVE ADJECTIVE	EXAMPLES
I	**my**	I'm a hard worker. **My** job is important.
you	**your**	You're a good teacher. **Your** class is fun.
he	**his**	He's an artist. **His** paintings are beautiful.
she	**her**	She's smart. **Her** parents are proud.
it	**its**	It's Emily's cat. **Its** fur is white.
we	**our**	We're excited. **Our** football team is in first place.
you	**your**	You're late. **Your** teachers are angry.
they	**their**	They're sad. **Their** friend is sick.

Questions with *Whose*		
WHOSE	NOUN	
Whose	car	is new?
	grades	are good?

Answers
Joe's.   **Joe's** car is new.
Tom's are.

Possessive Adjectives

- Possessive adjectives always come before nouns. They do not change form.

    His friend   **His** friends

- Possessive adjectives replace possessive nouns. They agree with the noun they replace.

    Juan's sister is in New York. = **His** sister is in New York.

            *Her sister is in New York. (INCORRECT)

⚠ Do not confuse the possessive adjective *its* with the contraction *it's*.

    Its fur is white.   **It's** friendly. (It is friendly.)

(Continued on page 104)

> **Questions with *Whose***
>
> - Use *whose* in information questions to ask about possession.
> - We can use *whose* without a noun if the meaning is clear.
>   **Whose** pen is this?   **Whose** is it?
>
> ⚠ Do not confuse *whose* with the contraction *who's*. They sound exactly the same.
>   **Whose** boyfriend is away at college?   **Who's** from Costa Rica? (Who is from Costa Rica?)

B1 Listening for Form

🎧 Listen to each sentence. Do you hear a possessive noun, a possessive adjective, or *whose*? Check (✓) the correct column.

	POSSESSIVE NOUN	POSSESSIVE ADJECTIVE	*WHOSE*
1.	✓		
2.			
3.			
4.			
5.			
6.			
7.			
8.			

B2 Working on Possessive Nouns

Complete the sentences with possessive nouns. Use the nouns in parentheses.

1. _Carol's_____ (Carol) book is on the table.

2. _____ (Brad and Jack) room is messy.

3. _____ (Mr. Miller) desk is in the corner.

4. The _____ (teachers) office is Room 432.

5. The _____ (Smiths) car is red.

6. The _____ (children) toy is broken.

7. _____ (Tamika) artwork is beautiful.

8. _____ (Sasha) garden is huge!

A. Form pairs of questions with *whose*. In the first question of each pair, use *whose* + noun. In the second question, use *whose* alone. Punctuate your sentences correctly.

1. **a.** major/whose/engineering/is <u>Whose major is engineering?</u>

   b. biology/whose/is <u>Whose is biology?</u>

2. **a.** car/whose/is/new _____

   b. old/whose/is _____

3. **a.** this month/whose/is/birthday _____

   b. next month/is/whose _____

4. **a.** whose/large/family/is _____

   b. is/whose/small _____

5. **a.** apartment/is/near school/whose _____

   b. far/is/whose _____

B. Work with a small group. Take turns asking and answering the questions in part A.

B4 Working on Possessive Adjectives

Complete the letter with the correct possessive adjective. Use the subject pronoun in parentheses to help you. Compare your answers with a partner.

Dear Keiko,

Good news! Jenny and I are finally in ___<u>our</u>___ (we) new house. The house
                                          1

isn't big but it's pretty. My best friend and _____ (he) wife are next door.
                                               2

_____ (they) son is in the same school as _____ (we) son.
     3   4

Jenny is happy because the house is near _____ (she) new office. John
                                           5

Bentley, _____ (she) boss, is a really nice guy. And guess what! _____
          6   7

(he) wife is the principal of _____ (we) daughter's new school!
                               8

How are you and _____ (you) family? Write soon!
                  9

                                              Paulo

Possessive Pronouns

Examining Form

Read the sentences and complete the tasks below. Then discuss your answers and read the Form charts to check them.

    a. My book isn't here. Mine is there.
    b. It isn't their dog. Theirs is black.

1. Underline the possessive adjectives + nouns.

2. A possessive pronoun replaces a possessive adjective + noun. Circle the possessive pronouns. What words do they replace?

Possessive Pronouns		
POSSESSIVE ADJECTIVE	POSSESSIVE PRONOUN	EXAMPLES
my	**mine**	My car isn't new. **Mine** is old.
your	**yours**	Your house isn't far. **Yours** is near.
his	**his**	His major isn't English. **His** is business.
her	**hers**	Her parents aren't Italian. **Hers** are Mexican.
Its		Its tail is short.
our	**ours**	Our class isn't difficult. **Ours** is easy.
your	**yours**	Your books aren't new. **Yours** are old.
their	**theirs**	Their families aren't in the United States. **Theirs** are in Mexico.

- A possessive pronoun replaces a possessive adjective + noun. Possessive pronouns are never followed by a noun.

    It's **my car.**   It's **mine.**   - *It's **mine** car. (INCORRECT)

- A possessive pronoun agrees with the possessive adjective that it replaces. Possessive pronouns have only one form.

    My book is red. — **Mine** is red.
    My books are red. — **Mine** are red.

Listening for Form

🎧 Listen to each sentence. Choose the word you hear.

1. **a.** your
   b. yours

2. **a.** his
   b. hers

3. **a.** our
   b. ours

4. **a.** yours
   b. your

5. **a.** your
   b. yours

6. **a.** their
   b. theirs

C2 **Forming Sentences with Possessive Pronouns**

Form sentences with possessive pronouns. Use the words and phrases. Punctuate your sentences correctly.

1. mine/the geology/book/is

   The geology book is mine.

2. the red/coat/yours/is

   _____

3. the tickets/his/are

   _____

4. the chocolate/theirs/is

   _____

5. is/the letter/ours

   _____

6. hers/are/the old/newspapers

   _____

C3 **Contrasting Possessive Pronouns and Possessive Adjectives**

Complete the conversation. Choose the correct word in parentheses.

Irina: Whose books are on my desk? Are they ((our)/ ours)$_1$ new books?

Robin: No, they're not (our / ours)$_2$. They're Kim's.

Irina: Why are they on (my / mine)$_3$ desk?

Robin: (Her / Hers)$_4$ desk is too crowded.

Irina: And the calculator? Is it (her / hers)$_5$?

Robin: No, it isn't. It's (my / mine)$_6$. Is the dictionary (your / yours)$_7$?

Irina: No, Robin. I think it's (your / yours)$_8$!

Possessives

Examining Meaning and Use

Read the sentences and answer the questions below. Then discuss your answers
and read the Meaning and Use Notes to check them.

a. My sister is a doctor. Keiko's sister is a teacher.
b. Their car is in the street. Mine is in the garage.
c. Mary's eyes are blue. Her brother's are green.

1. Underline the possessive forms.

2. Which sentence shows . . .

_____ ownership?

_____ a human relationship?

_____ a physical characteristic?

Meaning and Use Notes

Ownership and Possession

1 Possessive nouns, adjectives, and pronouns show that someone owns or
possesses something.

Erica's car is old.   **Her** car is old.   **Hers** is old.

John's homework is complete.   **His** homework is complete.   **His** is complete.

Human Relationships

2 Possessives show human relationships.

Yuki's mother is a doctor.   **Their** mother is a teacher.   **Mine** is a nurse.

Physical Characteristics

3 Possessives show physical characteristics.

Paul's hair is wavy.   **My** hair is black.   **Hers** is brown.

🎧 Listen to each sentence. Choose the correct statement.

1. **a.** Dan is 16 years old.
   b. Dan has a cat.
   c. I have a cat.

2. **a.** Karen is a doctor.
   b. Karen is in the hospital.
   c. Mr. Foster is sick.

3. **a.** Josh's grades are bad.
   b. Bob's and Josh's grades are good.
   c. Bob's grades aren't good.

4. **a.** Lynn is Robin's mother.
   b. Lynn is Larry's daughter.
   c. Larry is Robin's father.

5. **a.** I am in her house.
   b. She is in my house.
   c. He is in our house.

6. **a.** His car is new.
   b. Their car is new.
   c. Her car is new.

7. **a.** Paul's hair is black.
   b. Rick's hair is brown.
   c. Paul's hair is brown.

8. **a.** Irina's apartment is on Elm Street.
   b. My apartment is on Elm Street.
   c. My apartment is on Main Street.

D2 Describing Physical Characteristics ▶ Note 3

A. Work in pairs or small groups. Think of a person that everyone in your class knows, for example, a celebrity, a teacher, or a member of your class. Write three clues in your notebook to help your classmates guess the person's name. Use possessives.

1. *His eyes are blue.*
2. *His hair is brown.*
3. *His hair is short.*

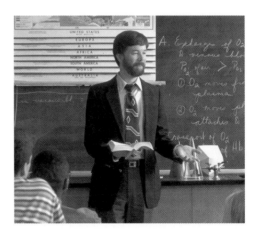

B. Work with another group. Take turns reading your clues. Ask your classmates to guess the person's name.

A: *His hair is short.*
B: *Is it our teacher?*

A. Complete the conversation. Use possessive forms of the words in parentheses. Think about the relationships between the family members.

Betty: What a nice photograph! Robin, is it ___yours___ (you)?
₁

Robin: Yes, it's _____ (me).
₂

Betty: Is this _____ (you) family?
₃

Robin: Well, it's _____ (Jim) family. This
₄

is Jim. He's _____ (I) husband.
₅

He's the man on the left. The woman

next to him is _____ (he) sister,
₆

Diane. The tall man in the hat is Diego, _____ (she) husband. And
₇

the boy next to him is _____ (they) son, Juan.
₈

Betty: Is the woman in the white dress _____ (Jim and Diane) mother?
₉

Robin: No, she's _____ (they) aunt Linda.
₁₀

Betty: What a beautiful house! Is it _____ (she) house?
₁₁

Robin: No, it's _____ (we) house . . . but thank you for the compliment!
₁₂

B. Read the conversation in part A again. Complete the sentences to express the relationships. Use possessive nouns.

1. Robin is ___Jim's___ wife.

2. Diane is _____ sister.

3. Diego is _____ husband.

4. Juan is _____ son.

5. Linda is _____ aunt.

6. Diane is _____ mother.

E # Demonstrative Adjectives and Demonstrative Pronouns

Examining Form

Read the sentences and complete the tasks below. Then discuss your answers and read the Form charts to check them.

1a. <u>This</u> desk is old. <u>That</u> desk is new.   **2a.** <u>This</u> book is mine. <u>That</u> is yours.
1b. <u>These</u> pens are blue. <u>Those</u> pens are red.   **2b.** <u>These</u> shoes are new. <u>Those</u> are old.

1. Look at the underlined adjectives in 1a and 1b. Which are singular? Which are plural? How do you know?

2. Look at the underlined words in 2a and 2b. Which are adjectives? Which are pronouns? How do you know?

DEMONSTRATIVE ADJECTIVES

Singular			
THIS/THAT	NOUN	VERB	
This	desk	is	new.
That			

Plural			
THESE/THOSE	NOUN	VERB	
These	desks	are	new.
Those			

DEMONSTRATIVE PRONOUNS

Singular		
THIS/THAT	VERB	
This	is	new.
That		

Plural		
THESE/THOSE	VERB	
These	are	new.
Those		

> **Demonstrative Adjectives and Pronouns**
> * *This, that, these,* and *those* are adjectives and pronouns.
> * When they come before singular and plural nouns, they are demonstrative adjectives.
>   **This** sports equipment is new.   **Those** books are old.

(Continued on page 112)

- When we use demonstratives without a noun, they are demonstrative pronouns.

  This is new.   **Those** are old.

- We usually use *it* or *they* in answers to *Yes/No* questions with demonstratives. We do not use *this, that, these,* or *those.*

  A: Is **that** shirt new?   A: Are **these** yours?

  B: No, **it** isn't.   B: Yes, **they** are.

- We often use demonstratives in questions with *whose.*

  Whose book bag is **this**?   Whose are **these**?

E1 **Listening for Form**

A. Listen to each sentence. Write the demonstrative (*this, that, these, those*) you hear.

1. _These_ socks are not mine. ((adjective)/ pronoun)

2. _____ books are interesting. (adjective / pronoun)

3. _____ tie is Alan's. (adjective / pronoun)

4. _____ is a beautiful painting. (adjective / pronoun)

5. _____ is my sister Wendy. (adjective / pronoun)

6. _____ are Jack's books, not mine. (adjective / pronoun)

B. Look at your answers in part A. Are they adjectives or pronouns? Choose the correct answer.

E2 **Building Sentences**

Build six logical sentences with demonstrative adjectives. Choose one word from each column, and write the sentences in your notebook. Punctuate your sentences correctly.

This dog is young.

this	children		young
that	dog	is	yours
these	pictures	are	a dormitory
those	building		small

Demonstratives

Examining Meaning and Use

Read the conversation and answer the questions below. Then discuss your answers and read the Meaning and Use Notes to check them.

> **Sally:** This is my telescope, and these are my astronomy books.
> **Brad:** What planet is that?
> **Sally:** That's Saturn. And those stars are the Pleiades.

1. Underline the demonstrative in each sentence.

2. Which demonstratives refer to objects near the speaker? Which refer to objects far from the speaker?

Meaning and Use Notes

People and Things

1 Demonstratives help a speaker identify people and things for a listener. We usually use them when both the speaker and the listener can see the people or objects. The speaker often points or gestures toward the object.

This house is cheap.

That house across the street is expensive.

These shoes are too small.

Those shoes next to the chair are fine.

Near and Far

2 *This* and *these* refer to people or things that are near the speaker. *That* and *those* refer to people or things that are far away.

Looking in a Mirror

This shirt is fine, but **these** pants are dirty.

Looking at the Sky

A: Look at **that** star!

B: **That's** not a star. It's the planet Venus.

A: Are **those** planets too?

Two Roommates Talking

A: Are **these** shoes OK?

B: No, don't wear **those**. Try **these**.

Listening for Meaning and Use　　　　► Notes 1, 2

🎧 Listen to each sentence. Is the noun near the speaker or far from the speaker? Check (✓) the correct column.

	NEAR	FAR
1.		✓
2.		
3.		
4.		
5.		
6.		

F2 **Talking About Near and Far Objects**　　　　► Notes 1, 2

A. Look at the objects. Write one true statement about each in your notebook. Use a demonstrative in each statement.

1.

These plants are healthy.

3.

5.

2.

4.

6.

B. Work with a partner. Find some of the objects in part A in your classroom. Make sentences about the objects. Use demonstratives.

Those plants are not healthy.

G # Combining Form, Meaning, and Use

G1 Thinking About Meaning and Use

Complete each conversation. Then discuss your answers in small groups.

1. **A:** Is this my book?

   B: _____
   - (a.) No, it's mine.
   - **b.** Yes, it's mine.
   - **c.** No, it's yours.

2. **A:** Is your aunt old?

   B: _____
   - **a.** No, you're young.
   - **b.** Yes, she is.
   - **c.** Yes, it is.

3. **A:** _____

   B: Mark's.
   - **a.** Who is Mark's teacher?
   - **b.** Whose teacher is that?
   - **c.** Who is that?

4. **A:** Is that dog yours?

   B: _____
   - **a.** No, it's Carl.
   - **b.** Yes, it's his.
   - **c.** No, it's not.

5. **A:** Is that your glass?

   B: _____
   - **a.** No, it's mine.
   - **b.** No, it's yours.
   - **c.** Yes, it's yours.

6. **A:** Is that their apartment?

   B: _____
   - **a.** No, it's theirs.
   - **b.** Yes, they are.
   - **c.** Yes, it is.

G2 Editing

Some of these sentences have errors. Find the errors and correct them.

1. ~~Mine~~ My house is white.

2. Her professors' family is from Mexico.

3. These are for you.

4. The records are mines.

5. Is this your or hers?

6. The university's library is very good.

7. Who's house is this?

8. Wash these dish.

▶ **Beyond the Classroom**

Searching for Authentic Examples

Look for advice columns in English-language newspapers and magazines, or on the Internet. Find at least three examples of possessive forms and three examples of demonstrative forms. Write them in your notebook. Explain to a partner why each one is a possessive or a demonstrative.

Speaking

Bring a photograph of your family or friends to class. Work in small groups. Take turns talking about the people in the photo. Describe their relationship to you. Ask questions about the people in the other students' photos.

A: *This is my family. This is my sister, Hanna, and this is my brother, Joon-ho.*
   These are my parents.
B: *Who is this woman?*
A: *That's my aunt. She's my father's sister.*

The Present

PART

4

The Present Continuous

People Watching

A1 Before You Read

Discuss these questions.

What is a journal? Do you write in a journal? What do you write about?

A2 Read

 Read this journal entry. What is the writer doing?

It's morning—my favorite time of day in Seattle. The city is waking up and I am too. I'm sitting in a small coffee shop. Outside, the weather is gloomy. It's cloudy, but it isn't raining. Two people are waiting at the bus stop. The woman is angry. She is pointing to her watch. She's complaining to the
5 man next to her. He isn't listening. He's reading his newspaper. A couple is sitting on a bench. They're about 25. The woman is wearing a waitress's uniform. The man is wearing a bus driver's uniform. They aren't talking. They are just holding hands and smiling at each other. I'm sure they are in love. Another couple is standing near them. They're both about 40.
10 They are carrying briefcases and wearing expensive clothes. They aren't talking; they aren't holding hands; and they aren't smiling. They are married—I'm sure. Are they fighting? Maybe. The woman is looking at the young couple. Perhaps she is thinking about happier times.

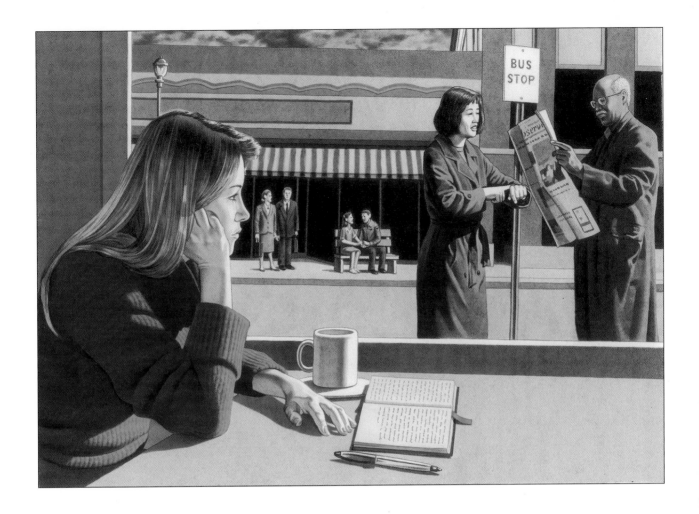

bench: a long seat for two or more people
complaining: expressing negative feelings about someone or something

couple: two people who have a romantic relationship
gloomy: dark and depressing
perhaps: maybe

A3 After You Read

Write *T* for true or *F* for false for each statement.

_F_ **1.** The writer is waiting for the bus.

____ **2.** The sun is shining.

____ **3.** A woman is complaining.

____ **4.** A woman is reading the newspaper.

____ **5.** A man and a woman are sitting on a bench.

____ **6.** Another couple is standing near the bench.

B The Present Continuous

Examining Form

Look back at the journal entry on page 120 and complete the tasks below. Then discuss your answers and read the Form charts to check them.

1. Look at the two underlined examples of the affirmative form of the present continuous. Each has two words. What are they?

2. Find three more affirmative examples of the present continuous.

3. Look at the circled examples of the negative form of the present continuous. Find three more negative examples.

Affirmative Statements		
SUBJECT	BE	BASE FORM OF VERB + -ING
I	am	
You	are	
He She It	is	waiting.
We		
You	are	
They		

CONTRACTIONS	
I'm	
You're	
He's	waiting.
They're	

Negative Statements			
SUBJECT	BE	NOT	BASE FORM OF VERB + -ING
I	am		
You	are		
He She It	is	not	waiting.
We			
You	are		
They			

CONTRACTIONS	
I'm not	
You're not You aren't	
He's not He isn't	waiting.
They're not They aren't	

- The contraction of *I* + *am* + *not* has only one form (**I'm not**).
- The contractions of all other subject pronouns + *be* + *not* have two possible forms. The meaning of these forms is the same.

    you **aren't** = you**'re** not   he **isn't** = he**'s** not

- See Appendix 3 for spelling rules for verbs ending in *-ing*.

Yes/No Questions

BE	SUBJECT	BASE FORM OF VERB + *-ING*
Am	I	
Are	you	
Is	she	
	we	**waiting?**
Are	you	
	they	

Short Answers

YES	SUBJECT	BE	NO	SUBJECT + BE + NOT
	you	are.		you **aren't**. you**'re not**.
	I	am.		I**'m not**.
	she	is.		she **isn't**. she**'s not**.
Yes,	you		No,	you **aren't**. you**'re not**.
	we	are.		we **aren't**. we**'re not**.
	they			they **aren't**. they**'re not**.

Information Questions

WH- WORD	BE	SUBJECT	BASE FORM OF VERB + *-ING*
How	am	I	**doing?**
What	are	you	
Who	is	he	**calling?**
Why	are	you	**waiting?**
Where		they	

WH- WORD (SUBJECT)	BE		BASE FORM OF VERB + *-ING*
Who	is		**talking?**
What			**cooking?**

Answers

Great.
I**'m cooking** dinner.
He**'s calling** David.
Because we missed the bus.
In the cafeteria.

Sasha.
Your dinner **is cooking**.

(Continued on page 124)

Yes/No Questions

⚠️ Do not use contractions in affirmative short answers.

Yes, **I am.**	Yes, **he is.**
*Yes, **I'm.** (INCORRECT)	*Yes, **he's.** (INCORRECT)

- Use either form of a negative contraction in negative short answers.

  No, you**'re** not. = No, you **aren't.**   No, she **isn't.** = No, she**'s not.**

- Negative short answers with the pronoun *I* have only one form.

  No, **I'm not.**

Information Questions

- It is not necessary to answer an information question with a complete sentence.

  A: Who is he calling?
  B: (He's calling) Amy.

- When *who* or *what* is the subject of the question, do not use a subject pronoun.

B1 Listening for Form

🎧 Listen to Mark and Gloria's telephone conversation. Choose the short answer you hear.

1. **a.** No, he's not
   (b.) No, I'm not.
   c. No, we aren't.

2. **a.** Yes, I am.
   b. Yes, it is.
   c. Yes, she is.

3. **a.** Yes, he is.
   b. Yes, it is.
   c. Yes, she is.

4. **a.** Yes, she is.
   b. Yes, he is.
   c. Yes, it is.

5. **a.** No, it's not.
   b. No, they're not.
   c. No, he's not.

6. **a.** Yes, he is.
   b. Yes, she is.
   c. Yes, it is.

7. **a.** No, it isn't.
   b. No, he isn't.
   c. No, it's not.

8. **a.** Yes, I am.
   b. Yes, we are.
   c. Yes, they are.

Complete each sentence with the present continuous form of the verb in parentheses.

1. He __is losing_____ (lose) the game.

2. I _____ (stop) for lunch.

3. She _____ (hug) her child.

4. We _____ (sit) on the couch.

5. They _____ (come) up the street.

6. You _____ (study) hard.

7. Paul and Susan _____ (exercise) at the gym.

8. Lee _____ (argue) with her sister.

Change the affirmative statements to negative statements. Rewrite the sentences in two different ways when possible.

1. It's raining right now.

   _It's not raining right now. It isn't raining right now._____

2. It's snowing in Maine.

   _____

3. The children are playing outside.

   _____

4. Celia is exercising at the gym.

   _____

5. I am fixing the car.

   _____

6. We are studying.

   _____

Complete the conversations with *Yes/No* questions. Use the words and phrases in parentheses and the present continuous. Punctuate your sentences correctly.

1. **A:** Excuse me. _Are you looking for something?_ (you/look for something)
   B: Yes. Where's the shampoo?

2. **A:** _____ (it/rain)
   B: No. The sun is shining.

3. **A:** _____ (I/pass the course)
   B: Yes, you are. In fact you are doing very well!

4. **A:** _____ (the kids/play outside)
   B: No, they're at the movies.

5. **A:** _____ (she/listen to a CD)
   B: No. She is playing the piano.

6. **A:** _____ (you/study Japanese)
   B: Yes. I'm taking classes at the community college.

Write information questions in your notebook about the underlined words in the statements. Punctuate your sentences correctly.

1. Reiko is reading <u>a magazine</u>.

   What is Reiko reading?

2. <u>Eva</u> is studying French.

3. Naomi is sitting <u>in the kitchen</u>.

4. Celia is drinking <u>coffee</u>.

5. Tom is feeling <u>fine</u>.

6. John's father is watching <u>television</u>.

The Present Continuous

Examining Meaning and Use

Read the sentences and answer the questions below. Then discuss your answers and read the Meaning and Use Notes to check them.

   a. **Julie:** Here, take your umbrella. <u>It's raining.</u>
       Paulo: Thanks. That's a good idea.

   b. **Steve:** Hi Carol. How are you?
       Carol: I'm very busy this week. <u>I'm writing a long research paper.</u>

1. Which underlined sentence talks about an activity that is in progress (happening) at the moment the speaker is talking?

2. Which underlined sentence talks about an activity that is in not happening at the moment the speaker is talking?

Activities in Progress

1A Use the present continuous to talk about activities that are in progress (happening) at the exact moment of speaking. Time expressions such as *now, right now,* and *at the moment* make the meaning clearer.

A: What **are** you **doing**?
B: **I'm studying** for my chemistry test.

A: How is the weather there in Michigan?
B: **It's snowing** <u>right now</u>.

1B Use the present continuous for activities that are in progress, but are not happening at the exact moment of speaking. Time expressions such as *still, these days, this week,* and *this semester* make the meaning clearer.

Two Former Classmates Meet on the Street
A: So, Rick, what **are** you **doing** <u>these days</u>?
B: **I'm** <u>still</u> **working** for my dad.

C1 Listening for Meaning and Use

► Notes 1A, 1B

Listen to the conversations. Which activities in progress are happening right now? Which are not happening right now? Check (✓) the correct column.

	HAPPENING RIGHT NOW	NOT HAPPENING RIGHT NOW
1.	✓	
2.		
3.		
4.		
5.		
6.		
7.		
8.		

C2 Describing Activities in Progress

► Note 1A

Look at the pictures. Then write a sentence in your notebook to describe each picture. Use contractions when possible.

1.

He's reading a newspaper.

3.

5.

2.

4.

6.

Talking About Activities in Progress but Not Right Now ► Note 1B

A. Read the list of activities. Put a check (✓) in the box for activities that you are doing these days. Put an ✗ in the box for activities that you are not doing these days.

	ACTIVITIES	✓/✗
1.	studying hard	
2.	working	
3.	playing a sport	
4.	dating someone	
5.	cooking dinner at home	
6.	planning a trip	
7.	dieting	
8.	learning to play an instrument	

B. Work with a partner. Ask and answer *Yes/No* questions and information questions about the information in part A.

A: What are you doing these days?
B: I'm studying hard.
A: Are you working, too?

C4 **Guessing Activities in Progress** ► Note 1A

Work in groups. Think of an activity, or use a suggestion from the list below. Act out the activity for the group, but don't say what activity you are doing. Your group asks *Yes/No* questions to guess what you are doing.

SUGGESTED ACTIVITIES	
riding a bicycle	arguing with your roommate
shopping	playing basketball
driving a truck	running a race

A: Are you riding a horse?
B: No, I'm not.

A: You are riding a bicycle!
B: Yes, I am.

Combining Sentences with *And*

We can use *and* to combine sentences. Use a comma when you combine two complete sentences.

> I am taking a shower. Alex is making dinner.
>
> I am taking a shower, **and** Alex is making dinner.

When two affirmative present continuous sentences have the same subject, we usually don't repeat the subject or *am/is/are*. In this case, we do not use a comma.

> **He** is doing his homework. **He** is watching television.
>
> **He** is doing his homework **and** watching television.

When we write, we combine sentences because it makes our writing sound more natural. Compare these two paragraphs.

A.	**B.**
Everyone in my family is very busy. My father is working out of town during the week. My father is coaching a soccer team on the weekends. My mother is teaching at the university. My mother is trying to start her own business. My brother Josh is going to law school. My brother Josh is working at a law firm.	Everyone in my family is very busy. My father is working out of town during the week **and** coaching a soccer team on the weekends. My mother is teaching at the university **and** trying to start her own business. My brother Josh is going to law school **and** working at a law firm.

C5 Combining Sentences with *And*

Rewrite the paragraph in your notebook. Use *and* to combine the underlined sentences. Punctuate your sentences correctly.

Dear Luisa,

Thanks for your letter. We're very busy, too. <u>We're working hard. We're saving money.</u> <u>Celia is teaching piano at the local high school. She's giving private lessons on the weekends.</u> <u>I'm finishing my Ph.D. I'm writing my dissertation.</u> <u>At the moment, Celia is making dinner. Our daughter Lucy is helping her.</u> . . .

Thanks for your letter. We're very busy, too. We're working hard and saving money. Celia . . .

D Combining Form, Meaning, and Use

D1 Thinking About Meaning and Use

Complete each conversation. Then discuss your answers in small groups.

1. **A:** Where is she going?

   B: _____
   - **a.** Now.
   - **(b.)** To the library.

2. **A:** Are you sleeping?

   B: _____
   - **a.** Yes, I'm studying.
   - **b.** No, I'm not.

3. **A:** Who is working with you?

   B: _____
   - **a.** Sara.
   - **b.** Now.

4. **A:** What are you looking at?

   B: _____
   - **a.** It's snowing.
   - **b.** It's snowing these days.

5. **A:** What are you doing these days?

   B: _____
   - **a.** I'm taking a bath.
   - **b.** I'm looking for a new job.

6. **A:** Is the baby crying?

   B: _____.
   - **a.** No, not now.
   - **b.** Yes, this week.

D2 Editing

Find the errors in this letter and correct them.

Dear Gina,

    standing

I'm ~~stand~~ in front of your apartment. Unfortunately, you're not at home, so

I writing you this note. Dan and I are visiting our families. We're live in San Diego

now. Dan working for a telecommunications company, and I'm looking for a job.

What you are doing these days? Are you still write for the newspaper? Call me at

my mother's house and please visit us!

           Miss you,

           Holly

▶ Beyond the Classroom

Searching for Authentic Examples

Watch an English-language movie or TV program. Listen for the present continuous. Write six examples in your notebook and share them with your class. Why do you think the sentences are in the present continuous?

Writing

Follow the steps below to write a paragraph about activities and events that you see at a public place.

1. Go to a restaurant, a coffee shop, a shopping center, a park, or somewhere where you can watch people. Use these questions to make notes.

   - Where are you?
   - What are you doing?
   - What are other people doing?
   - Where are they going?

2. Write a first draft. Use the present continuous to describe the activities you see.

3. Read your work carefully and circle grammar, spelling, and punctuation errors. Work with a partner to decide how to fix the errors and improve the content.

4. Rewrite your draft.

   I'm sitting in a park. A man is reading the newspaper and eating a sandwich. . . .

The Simple Present

A Career Path Asks: "What Do You Do?"

A1 Before You Read

Discuss these questions.

Do you work and go to school? Do you know anyone who works and goes to school? Is it easy or difficult to work and go to school? Why?

A2 Read

Read this magazine interview with Kyla Adams. What makes Kyla an unusual student?

CAREER PATH

Career Path Asks "What Do You Do?"
Interviews with students with unusual lives

Every month *Career Path* magazine interviews a student with an unusual life. This month Kyla Adams is our unusual student. Kyla is a very busy young woman. She is a student, and she dances for the Ballet Tech Company in New York City. Read what Kyla says to our interviewer.

5 ***Career Path:*** How many hours a day do you dance?

Kyla: A lot. I have ballet class from 10:30 to 12:00. Then we rehearse from 10 12:00 to 3:30 and 4:30 to 6:00.

Career Path: What do you do after rehearsal?

Kyla: I'm usually very 15 tired. I go home and make dinner. Then I study or read and go to bed.

Career Path: Who do you live with?

20 **Kyla:** I live alone. I have a tiny apartment in Manhattan.

Career Path: Where does your family live?

25 **Kyla:** They're about four hours away in Vermont.

Career Path: Do you get lonely?

Kyla: No. I have a lot of 30 friends. They call or visit a lot.

Career Path: Does your family visit you?

Kyla: Oh yes. They come 35 here, or I go home twice a month.

Career Path: You are still in high school. Who teaches you?

40 **Kyla:** I have a tutor for a couple of classes. For my other classes, I work by myself. But I communicate with 45 students in my home high school on the telephone and the computer.

Career Path: When do 50 you study?

Kyla: On Sundays. That's my day off. We have three weeks of vacation a year. I study a lot then, too.

55 **Career Path:** How are you doing in school?

Kyla: Very well. I'm actually the valedictorian of my high school class.

60 **Career Path:** What do you do in your free time?

Kyla: I don't have much free time. But I live in New York City, so it's not 65 hard to find things to do.

---

rehearse: to practice
rehearsal: a practice for a show or performance

tutor: a private teacher who teaches one person
valedictorian: the student who receives the best grades in his or her high school class

---

A3 **After You Read**

Write *T* for true or *F* for false for each statement. Change the false statements to true ones.

___F___ **1.** Kyla rehearses from 10:30 to 12:00.

Kyla rehearses from 12:00 to 3:30 and 4:30 to 6:00.

_____ **2.** Kyla lives with a friend.

_____ **3.** Kyla's family lives in New York.

_____ **4.** Kyla doesn't get lonely.

_____ **5.** Kyla communicates with other students by phone.

_____ **6.** Kyla doesn't have a lot of free time.

B Simple Present Statements

Examining Form

Read the sentences and complete the tasks below. Then discuss your answers and read the Form charts to check them.

1a. I come home at six o'clock.
1b. She comes home at three o'clock.
1c. They come home at eight o'clock.

2a. I do not walk to work.
2b. He does not walk to work
2c. They do not walk to work.

1. Sentences 1a–1c are affirmative. Circle the subjects and underline the verbs. What is different about the form of the verb in 1b?

2. Sentences 2a–2c are negative. Circle the subjects. What three words come after each subject? What is different about the form of the negative verb in 2b?

3. Look back at the interview on pages 134–135. Find three affirmative sentences and one negative sentence.

Affirmative Statements		
SUBJECT	**BASE FORM OF VERB or BASE FORM OF VERB + -S/-ES**	
I	**live**	
You		
He She It	**lives**	in Texas.
We		
You	**live**	
They		

Negative Statements			
SUBJECT	**DO/DOES + NOT**	**BASE FORM OF VERB**	
I	**do not don't**		
You			
He She It	**does not doesn't**	**live**	in Texas.
We	**do not don't**		
You			
They			

- To form the simple present, use the base form of the verb. In the third-person singular (*he, she,* or *it*), add -*s* or -*es* to the base form.

  He **works** hard.   She **teaches** math.

- See Appendix 4 for spelling rules for verbs ending in -*s* or -*es*.

- *Have* is an irregular verb. The third-person singular form of *have* is *has*.

  I **have** a new car.   He **has** a new car.

- To form negative statements, use *do/does* + *not* + the base form of the verb. Only use *does not (doesn't)* in the third-person singular *(he, she,* or *it)*.

  He **does not work** hard.   She **doesn't teach** math.

- We usually use the contractions *don't* and *doesn't* in speaking and informal writing.

- ⚠ In negative statements, do not add -*s* or -*es* to the base form of the verb in the third-person singular.

  He **does not play** golf.

  *He does not plays golf. (INCORRECT)

B1 Listening for Form

🎧 Listen to each sentence about Kyla Adams. Choose the affirmative or negative form of the verb you hear.

1. **a.** live
   b. lives
   c. doesn't live

2. **a.** has
   b. have
   c. doesn't have

3. **a.** has
   b. have
   c. doesn't have

4. **a.** dance
   b. dances
   c. doesn't dance

5. **a.** study
   b. studies
   c. doesn't study

6. **a.** worry
   b. worries
   c. doesn't worry

7. **a.** miss
   b. misses
   c. doesn't miss

8. **a.** work
   b. works
   c. doesn't work

B2 Working on Simple Present Affirmative Statements

Complete the paragraph. Use the correct simple present form of the verb in parentheses.

Lisa and Alan ___work___ (work) in a bank. Lisa _____ (live) with her
1   2

parents. Alan _____ (share) an apartment with his brother. Lisa and Alan
3

are good friends. They _____ (drive) to work together in Alan's car. Lisa
4

_____ (have) a job in the bank's loan department, and Alan _____ (fix)
5   6

the bank's computers. They _____ (finish) work at 5:00 P.M. After work, Lisa
7

_____ (go) to the gym and _____ (exercise). Alan _____ (drive)
8   9   10

home alone. He and his brother _____ (watch) the six o'clock news. Then they
11

_____ (make) dinner.
12

B3 Contrasting Simple Present Affirmative and Negative Statements

Make the false statements true by changing them to negative statements. Then
write a true affirmative statement. Use the words in parentheses in place of the
underlined words.

1. Tigers have spots. (stripes)

   Tigers don't have spots. They have stripes.

2. Trees lose their leaves in the summer. (fall)

   _____

3. The moon goes around the sun. (earth)

   _____

4. Panda bears eat bananas. (bamboo)

   _____

5. An astronomer studies the ocean. (stars)

   _____

6. Water boils at 100°F. (212°F)

   _____

Pronunciation Notes

Pronunciation of Verbs Ending in -s and -es

The final -s or -es of third-person singular verbs has three pronunciations: /s/, /z/, and /ɪz/. The pronunciation depends on the final sound of the base form of the verb.

1. If the base form of the verb ends with the sound /p/, /t/, /k/, or /f/, pronounce -s or -es as /s/.

   stop — stops   /stɑps/   like — likes   /laɪks/
   meet — meets   /mits/   laugh — laughs   /læfs/

2. If the base form of the verb ends with the sound /b/, /d/, /g/, /v/, /ð/, /m/, /n/, /ŋ/, /l/, or /r/, pronounce -s or -es as /z/.

   build — builds   /bɪldz/   ring — rings   /rɪŋz/
   leave — leaves   /livz/   tell — tells   /tɛlz/

3. If the base form of the verb ends in a vowel sound, pronounce -s or -es as /z/.

   stay — stays   /steɪz/   go — goes   /goʊz/
   see — sees   /siz/   fly — flies   /flaɪz/

4. If the base form of the verb ends with the sound /s/, /z/, /ʃ/, /ʒ/, /tʃ/, /dʒ/, or /ks/, pronounce -es as /ɪz/. This adds an extra syllable to the word.

   wash — washes   /ˈwɑʃɪz/   judge — judges   /ˈdʒʌdʒɪz/
   catch — catches   /ˈkætʃɪz/   fix — fixes   /ˈfɪksɪz/

B4) Pronouncing the Third-Person -s and -es

🎧 Listen to each verb alone and in a sentence. What final sound do you hear? Check (✓) the correct column.

		/s/	/z/	/ɪz/
1.	speaks	✓		
2.	smells			
3.	washes			
4.	leaves			
5.	notices			
6.	stops			
7.	pays			
8.	teaches			

C Simple Present *Yes/No* Questions and Short Answers

Examining Form

Read these sentences and complete the tasks below. Then discuss your answers and read the Form charts to check them.

   a. Do you like spinach?
   b. Does she watch TV every day?
   c. Do they have a lot of homework?

1. Circle the subject in each question. What word comes before each subject?

2. What is different about sentence b?

3. Underline the verb form that follows each subject. Do we add an ending to the verb?

Yes/No Questions		
DO/DOES	**SUBJECT**	**BASE FORM OF VERB**
Do	I	
	you	
Does	he she it	**work?**
Do	we	
	you	
	they	

Short Answers					
YES	**SUBJECT**	**DO/DOES**	**NO**	**SUBJECT**	**DO/DOES + NOT**
Yes,	you	**do.**	**No,**	you	**don't.**
	I			I	
	he she it	**does.**		he she it	**doesn't.**
	you	**do.**		you	**don't.**
	we			we	
	they			they	

> - Use *does* for the third-person singular.
> ⚠ In *Yes/No* questions, do not add *-s* or *-es* to the base form in the third-person singular.
>   Does he **work** here?
>   * Does he **works** here? (INCORRECT)

🎧 Listen to the conversation between Sally and her father. Choose the answer you hear.

1. a. Yes, she does.
   b. Yes, it does.
   (c.) No, I don't.

2. a. Yes, I do.
   b. Yes, he does.
   c. No, it doesn't.

3. a. Yes, I do.
   b. Yes, it does.
   c. No, it doesn't.

4. a. No, she doesn't.
   b. Yes, they do.
   c. Yes, we do.

5. a. Yes, you do.
   b. Yes, we do.
   c. No, I don't.

6. a. No, she doesn't.
   b. No, he doesn't.
   c. No, I don't.

7. a. Yes, we do.
   b. No, they don't.
   c. No, we don't.

8. a. Yes, I do.
   b. Yes, they do.
   c. No, I don't.

C2 Working on Simple Present *Yes/No* Questions

A. Complete the questions with *do* or *does*.

1. _Do_____ you like ethnic food?

2. _____ you go to jazz clubs?

3. _____ you exercise?

4. _____ you dislike violence on television?

5. _____ classical music relax you?

6. _____ you read many books?

7. _____ science interest you?

8. _____ your best friend live with you?

B. Work with two other students. Take turns asking and answering the questions in part A.

A: Do you like ethnic food?
B: Yes, I do.

A. Look at the class schedules and complete the *Yes/No* questions below. Use *do* or *does*.

Lightman College
Winter Term

Name: Diego Florez
Address: Cherry Hill Dorm
          Lightman College

Schedule

Biology 101	M–F 9:00–11:00
Chemistry 1	Tu, Thu 2:30–5:00
Italian 101	M–F 12:45–1:30
Basketball	Sat 9:00–11:00

Lightman College
Winter Term

Name: Amy Lim
Address: Grandview Dorm
          Lightman College

Schedule

Biology 101	M–F 9:00–11:00
Chemistry 1	Tu, Thu 2:30–5:00
German 101	M–F 12:45–1:30

1. __Does__ Diego study biology?

2. _____ Amy go to Chemistry 1 on Fridays?

3. _____ Diego and Amy live on campus?

4. _____ German 101 meet on Wednesdays?

5. _____ Biology 101 start at 10:00?

6. _____ Diego play football?

7. _____ Diego and Amy study accounting?

8. _____ Amy have a class on Tuesday morning?

B. Look at the class schedules again, and answer the questions in part A. Use short answers.

1. __Yes, he does.__   5. _____

2. _____   6. _____

3. _____   7. _____

4. _____   8. _____

D Simple Present Information Questions

Examining Form

Read the sentences and complete the tasks below. Then discuss your answers and read the Form charts to check them.

1a. Do you live here?   **2a.** Does she study in the evening?
1b. Where do you live?   **2b.** When does she study?

1. Which sentences are *Yes/No* questions? Which are information questions?

2. How do *Yes/No* questions begin? How do information questions begin?

Information Questions					Answers
WH- WORD	*DO/DOES*	SUBJECT	BASE FORM OF VERB		
Who	do	I	call	for help?	Call your teacher.
What		you	read?		Novels.
Where	does	he	live?		He **lives** in the dorm.
		she			In Chicago.
When		we	eat	dinner?	At 7:00 every day.
Why	do	you	exercise?		For my health.
How		they	play?		They **play** well.

WH- WORD (SUBJECT)	BASE FORM OF VERB + -*S*/-*ES*				
Who	lives		in Texas?		My father **does**.
What	smells		good?		Dinner.

⚠ When *who* or *what* is the subject of a question, do not use *do* or *does* or a subject pronoun
   Who **cleans** the kitchen?   * Who does she clean the kitchen? (INCORRECT)

D1) Listening for Form

🎧 Listen to the questions. Write the words you hear.

1. _Where do_ you live?

2. _____ lives with you?

3. _____ you get to work?

4. _____ you eat lunch?

5. _____ you do on Saturday morning?

6. _____ the shopping?

7. _____ he go shopping?

8. _____ happens on Saturday night?

D2) Working on Information Questions

A. Read the statements. Write information questions about the underlined words or phrases.

1. Linda's father works <u>in a bank on Main Street.</u>

    Where does Linda's father work?

2. Lee's brother studies <u>medicine.</u>

    _____

3. Lynn and Paulo begin work <u>at 8:00 A.M.</u>

    _____

4. Larry drives <u>carefully.</u>

    _____

5. <u>Greg</u> drives his car to work.

    _____

6. Koji takes a bus <u>because he doesn't have a car.</u>

    _____

B. Work with a partner. Take turns asking and answering information questions with the phrases below.

go home   live   study   eat lunch

A: *How do you go home?*
B: *I take a bus.*

A. Look at the pictures. Read the job descriptions and match them to the pictures.

a.

c.

e.

b.

d.

f.

___e___ **1.** A magician performs magic tricks.

_____ **2.** A surgeon performs surgery.

_____ **3.** An auto mechanic repairs cars.

_____ **4.** A pastry chef bakes cakes, cookies, and other sweets.

_____ **5.** A dog walker takes other people's dogs for walks.

_____ **6.** An optician makes and sells eyeglasses.

B. Write one *Who* and one *What* question for each job description.

Who performs magic tricks?
What does a magician do?

C. Work with a partner. Take turns asking and answering your *Who* and *What* questions in part B.

A: Who performs magic tricks?
B: A magician.

The Simple Present

Examining Meaning and Use

Read the sentences and answer the questions below. Then discuss your answers and read the Meaning and Use Notes to check them.

a. Los Angeles has over 3 million people.
b. My mother makes spaghetti every Sunday.
c. The word *enormous* means "very big."

1. Which sentence talks about a habit or routine (something that happens again and again)?

2. Which sentence gives a definition?

3. Which sentence gives factual information (that you can find in a book)?

4. Which verb expresses an action?

Meaning and Use Notes

Habits and Routines

1 Use the simple present to talk about habits and routines (things that happen again and again).

A: How **does** your father **get** to work?   A: What **do** you **do** in your free time?
B: He **takes** the train.   B: I **read** and **paint**.

Factual Information

2 Use the simple present to talk about factual information, such as general truths, definitions, and scientific facts.

General Truths   *Scientific Facts*
Most cars **use** gasoline for fuel.   Water **freezes** at 32°F.

Definitions
A: What does *rehearse* **mean**?
B: It **means** "to practice."

Stative Verbs and the Simple Present

3 Stative verbs do not express actions. They express states and conditions such as physical descriptions, senses, possessions, measurements, feelings, and knowledge. We often use stative verbs in the simple present to express these states and conditions.

Descriptions	*Possessions*	*Feelings*
She **looks** beautiful.	Joe **owns** a motorcycle.	I **dislike** loud music.
The house **is** empty.	The book **belongs** to Ann.	They **love** each other.
Senses	*Measurements*	*Knowledge*
The flowers **smell** sweet.	The book **costs** $9.95.	She **understands** Thai.
The soup **tastes** good.	He **weighs** 139 pounds.	We **know** the answer.

⚠️ We do not usually use stative verbs in the present continuous.

He **understands** that now.   The weather **seems** cold.

*He is understanding that now.   *The weather is seeming cold.
    (INCORRECT)   (INCORRECT)

E1 **Listening for Meaning and Use**   ▶ Notes 1–3

 Listen to the questions and answers. What are they about? Check (✓) the correct column.

	HABITS AND ROUTINES	FACTUAL INFORMATION	FEELINGS AND SENSES
1.	✓		
2.			
3.			
4.			
5.			
6.			
7.			
8.			

A. Describe Naomi and Alex's weekend routine. Use the verbs below.

call	cook	dance	go	make	take
clean	correct	give	eat	shop	watch

On Saturday mornings, Alex

____cooks____ breakfast and Naomi
         1

_____ a list of all their weekend
      2

activities. Then they _____ the
                            3

house. On Saturday afternoons, Alex

_____ for the week's groceries
      4

at the supermarket and Naomi

_____ her students' homework. On Saturday evenings, they _____ to
      5   6

their favorite club and _____ until after midnight.
                              7

On Sunday mornings, Alex and Naomi _____ a late breakfast. Then they
                                          8

_____ their parents. On Sunday afternoons, they _____ a long walk
      9   10

in the park with their dog. In the evening, Naomi _____ the dog a bath
                                                        11

and Alex _____ a football game on TV.
              12

B. Write six information questions about Naomi and Alex's routine in your notebook.

Who cooks breakfast on Saturday morning?

C. Work with a partner. Take turns asking and answering your questions in part B.

A: Who cooks breakfast on Saturday mornings?
B: Alex does. Who makes a list of all their weekend activities?

Beyond the Sentence

Linking Ideas in the Simple Present

Use sequence words such as *first, then, next, after that,* and *finally* when you describe actions in a sequence. Compare the two paragraphs below.

Without Sequence Words	*With Sequence Words*
On Saturdays I get up at nine o'clock. I take a shower. I eat breakfast and read the newspaper. I wash the dishes. I go shopping.	On Saturdays I get up at nine o'clock. **First** I take a shower. **Then** I eat breakfast and read the newspaper. **Next** I wash the dishes. **After** that, I go shopping.

E3 Linking Ideas with Sequence Words

A. Complete the chart. Write some things you do on a Monday morning and some things you do on a Monday afternoon.

MONDAY MORNING	MONDAY AFTERNOON
I get up early.	

B. Use the chart from part A to write two paragraphs about your typical Monday. In the first paragraph, describe your morning activities. In the second paragraph, describe your afternoon activities. Use a sequence word to introduce each new activity.

On a typical Monday morning, I get up at 6:00 A.M. First I take a shower and brush my teeth. Then I get dressed. . . .

E4) Describing Jobs ► Notes 1–3

A. Read the paragraph. In your notebook, write a question for each underlined word or phrase.

<u>Archeologists</u> study societies of the past. They examine <u>the remains of ancient</u>
   1

<u>buildings and graves</u>. They dig <u>very slowly and carefully</u>. Their job is difficult
                                   3

<u>because they work in all weather conditions</u>. Nautical archeologists work
          4

<u>under water</u>. They use <u>special diving equipment and digging tools</u> in their work.
   5   6

Who studies past societies?

B. Write three to five sentences about one of the jobs below. Look in a dictionary or encyclopedia for help. Use the description in part A as a model.

paleontologist   meteorologist   entomologist

A paleontologist studies fossils. . .

E5) Writing a Description ► Note 3

A. Complete this description. Use the correct form of the stative verbs below.

feel   hate   have   have   live   look   love   weigh

Susan Acosta ___lives___ in Seattle with her family. She is married and
               1

_____ three children. During the week, she is a wife and mother. On the
    2

weekends, she is a long distance runner. Susan is 40 years old, but she

_____ young for her age. She _____ light brown hair and green
   3   4

eyes. She is 5 feet 2 inches tall, and she _____ only 100 pounds. Susan is
                                   5

very fit. She exercises every day, and she runs in three marathons every year.

Susan _____ her sport, but she _____ competition. "Before a race,
      6   7

I _____ very nervous. I don't like it, but it helps me run fast!"
  8

B. Write a description of a friend or a family member. Use the description in part A as a model. Write five or six sentences. Use a variety of stative verbs.

My brother Chang looks very young for his age. He is six feet tall and thin. He is a law student . . .

Combining Form, Meaning, and Use

Thinking About Meaning and Use

Complete each conversation. Then discuss your answers in small groups.

1. **A:** _____

   B: In Florida.
   - **a.** Where do you live?
   - **b.** Who do you live with?
   - **c.** What do you do?

2. **A:** _____ after work?

   B: To the gym.
   - **a.** Where does she
   - **b.** Where she goes
   - **c.** Where does she go

3. **A:** Does Steve clean the house?

   B: _____
   - **a.** Yes, he is.
   - **b.** No. I do.
   - **c.** Yes, we do.

4. **A:** Who teaches your class?

   B: _____
   - **a.** A class of fifth graders.
   - **b.** A woman from Spain.
   - **c.** Spanish.

5. **A:** _____

   B: It cools the air.
   - **a.** What does an air conditioner do?
   - **b.** Who makes an air conditioner?
   - **c.** What is an air conditioner?

6. **A:** What does your brother look like?

   B: _____
   - **a.** He likes soccer.
   - **b.** He has dark hair.
   - **c.** He looks for his shoes.

7. **A:** Who owns that bicycle?

   B: _____
   - **a.** Ted is.
   - **b.** Ted does.
   - **c.** Ted has.

8. **A:** Does water freeze at 212° F?

   B: No. It _____ at 32° F.
   - **a.** is freezing
   - **b.** freezes
   - **c.** freeze

Find the errors in this paragraph and correct them.

Sun-hee ~~go~~ *goes* to a college in Southern California. This is her freshman year, and

everything seem new and exciting to her. After three months at the college, she have

many friends and don't feel lonely. She works hard and get good grades, but she

also enjoy life with her friends. On Saturday mornings, they studies together at the

library, but in the afternoons they take long walks or doing other outdoor activities.

Sunday morning is her favorite part of the week. Her friends sleep late on Sundays,

but Sun-hee get up at 7:00 and goes horseback riding in a forest near the college.

▶ Beyond the Classroom

Searching for Authentic Examples

Look for an interview in an English-language newspaper or magazine, or on the
Internet. Find six questions in the simple present. Write them in your notebook
and share them with your class. Why does the writer use the simple present?

Writing

Follow the steps below to write an interview with a friend or classmate.

1. Interview a friend or a classmate. Write three *Yes/No* questions and three
   information questions about his or her daily routine. For example:

   What time do you get up?   *How do you get to school?*

2. Use the questions to interview your friend. Write his or her answers.

3. Write a first draft. Use the simple present.

4. Read your work carefully and circle grammar, spelling, and punctuation errors.
   Work with a partner to decide how to fix the errors and fix the content.

5. Rewrite your draft.

   Interviewer: What time do you get up in the morning?
   Paulo: I get up at 7:00 A.M.
   Interviewer: How do you get to school?
   Paulo: I take the bus to the park. Then I walk.

Adverbs of Frequency

A What Kind of Learner Are You?

A1 Before You Read

Discuss these questions.

Do you like to listen to lectures? Do you prefer to look at pictures and diagrams?
Do you like to do experiments? Do you think everyone learns in the same way?

A2 Read

Read the article from a science magazine on the following page. What kind of
learner are you?

A3 After You Read

Write *T* for true or *F* for false for each statement.

___T___ **1.** Teachers like good listeners.

_____ **2.** Good listeners don't always follow instructions.

_____ **3.** Julie Hong does well in school.

_____ **4.** Larry Dawson is good with details.

_____ **5.** Hands-on learners don't usually learn from books.

_____ **6.** Pete Donaldson spends a lot of time on the computer.

What Kind of Learner Are You?

Researchers say that there are at least three different types of learners.

Some learners are good listeners. Teachers like them because they always 5 follow instructions. Julie Hong is a student like this. She gets A's in all her classes at Deerfield High School in 10 Connecticut. She loves school, and her teachers love her because she always pays attention in class. "I pay attention because I don't want to miss important information," she says.

15 Some people learn from pictures and diagrams. They are very creative but don't like details. 20 Larry Dawson is a good example of this kind of learner. He is studying graphic design at Warfield Community College in Ohio.

25 He is usually very good with ideas and concepts but sometimes has problems with details. "New ideas are exciting, but I often get bored at the end of a big project," Larry admits.

30 Some learners rarely learn from books or pictures. They are "hands-on" learners. They learn from 35 experience. Pete Donaldson is a good example of a hands-on learner. Pete is studying computer science at the University of Florida. 40 Pete never reads computer manuals and seldom looks at diagrams. He just spends hours on the computer. "That's the best way for me to learn," he says.

So, what kind of learner are you?

45 Do you always learn the same way? Or do you learn one way in some classes and another way in others?

---

concepts: ideas or principles
creative: using skill or imagination to make new things
details: small facts or pieces of information

hands-on: learned by doing, not watching
manuals: books that explain how to do something
pay attention: listen to something or someone carefully

B Adverbs of Frequency

Examining Form

Read the sentences and complete the tasks below. Then discuss your answers and read the Form charts to check them.

    a. Good listeners are usually good learners.
    b. They always follow instructions.
    c. Some learners are often bad with details.
    d. Some learners rarely read books.

1. We use adverbs of frequency to say how often something happens. Underline the adverb of frequency in each sentence.

2. Look at the sentences with the verb *be*. Is the adverb of frequency before or after *be*?

3. Look at the sentences with other verbs. Is the adverb of frequency before or after the verb?

Affirmative Statements with *Be*			
SUBJECT	***BE***	**ADVERB**	
I	am		
She	is	**always** **seldom**	late.
We	are		

Affirmative Statements with Other Verbs			
SUBJECT	**ADVERB**	**VERB**	
I		walk	
She	**always** **seldom**	walks	home.
We		walk	

Negative Statements with *Be*			
SUBJECT	**ADVERB**	***BE + NOT***	
I		am not	
She	**generally** **usually**	isn't	late.
We		aren't	

Negative Statements with Other Verbs				
SUBJECT	**ADVERB**	***DO/DOES + NOT***	**VERB**	
I		don't		
She	**generally** **usually**	doesn't	walk	home.
We		don't		

Yes/No Question with *Be*				Answers
BE	SUBJECT	ADVERB		
Is	he	**always**	happy?	Yes. Yes, he is. Yes, he **generally** is.

Yes/No Question with Other Verbs				Answers
DO/DOES	SUBJECT	ADVERB	BASE FORM OF VERB	
Do	you	**usually**	exercise?	No. No, I don't. No, I **never** do.

Adverbs of Frequency

- Use adverbs of frequency to say how often something happens.
- Adverbs of frequency can be positive or negative.

Positive Adverbs	*Negative Adverbs*
always, almost always,	rarely, seldom,
frequently, usually,	hardly ever,
generally, often,	almost never,
sometimes, occasionally	never

⚠ Do not use negative adverbs of frequency in negative statements.
We rarely eat lunch.   * We don't rarely eat lunch. (INCORRECT)

Placement of Adverbs of Frequency

- In affirmative statements, adverbs of frequency come after the verb *be*. They come before other verbs.
- In negative statements, most adverbs of frequency come before *be + not* or *do + not*.
- However, *always* comes after *be + not* or *do + not*.
  She <u>isn't</u> **always** late.   She <u>doesn't</u> **always** eat lunch.
- In *Yes/No* questions and short answers, adverbs of frequency come after the subject.

Other Positions of Adverbs of Frequency

- *Frequently, usually, generally, sometimes,* and *occasionally* can also come at the beginning or end of a sentence.
  Sometimes I'm late.   I don't eat lunch **usually**.

🎧 Listen to the description. Write the adverbs of frequency you hear.

Some adults ___*occasionally*___
                              1
get very angry when they drive.

Experts call this "road rage." Road rage

is dangerous because angry drivers

_____ drive carelessly
         2

and _____ cause
            3

accidents. These drivers

_____ care about other drivers. They are _____
         4   5

rude and hostile. Angry drivers _____ drive very fast, and they
                                               6

_____ shout at other drivers.
         7

B2 **Forming Sentences with Adverbs of Frequency**

Form sentences with adverbs of frequency in your notebook. Use the words and phrases. There may be more than one correct order. Punctuate your sentences correctly. Compare your sentences with a partner.

1. Lisa/gets angry/often

   Lisa often gets angry.

2. don't/watch TV/usually/I

3. is/always/on time/she/

4. rarely/eats lunch/Rick

5. work late/don't/we/generally

6. drinks coffee/she/never

Read the sentences. Write new sentences using the adverbs of frequency in parentheses. There may be more than one position for the adverb.

1. Jack is very slow in the morning. (frequently)

   Jack is frequently very slow in the morning. OR Frequently, Jack is

   very slow in the morning.

2. He needs a lot of time to get ready. (always)

   _____

3. He spends 30 minutes in the shower. (almost always)

   _____

4. He is on time for work. (never)

   _____

5. He stays out late with his friends. (usually)

   _____

6. He goes to bed before 2:00 A.M. (rarely)

   _____

B4) **Forming *Yes/No* Questions with Adverbs of Frequency**

A. Form *Yes/No* questions with adverbs of frequency in your notebook. Use the words and phrases. Punctuate your sentences correctly.

   1. you/usually/on time/are

      Are you usually on time?

   2. always/do/your friends/remember your birthday

   3. you/almost always/do/do your homework

   4. generally/you/are/in a good mood

   5. usually/the bus/take/you/do/to school

   6. sometimes/you and your friends/go to the movies/do

B. Work with a small group. Take turns asking and answering the questions in part A.

C **Adverbs of Frequency**

Examining Meaning and Use

Read the sentences and complete the tasks below. Then discuss your answers and read the Meaning and Use Notes to check them.

a. Bob usually does his homework. He's an average student.
b. Ana rarely does her homework. She gets in trouble with her teacher.
c. Mike never does his homework. He's failing the class.
d. Teresa always does her homework. She's an excellent student.

Underline the adverbs of frequency in the sentences above. How often do these people do their homework? Write the letter of each sentence on the correct line of the chart below.

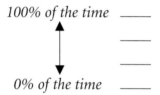

100% of the time _____
_____
_____
0% of the time _____

Meaning and Use Notes

Common Adverbs of Frequency

1A We use adverbs of frequency to express how often something happens.

100% • always
• almost always
• frequently, often
• usually, generally
• sometimes, occasionally
• rarely, seldom
• almost never, hardly ever
0% • never

1B We can use other frequency expressions such as *all the time, some of the time,* and *once in a while* instead of certain adverbs of frequency. These frequency expressions usually go at the end of the sentence.

I am **always** busy. = I am busy <u>all the time</u>.
She **sometimes** walks to work. = She walks to work <u>some of the time</u>.
They **occasionally** visit me. = They visit me <u>once in a while</u>.

2 These adverbs of frequency have opposite meanings.

Always / Never
He **always** tells the truth. He **never** lies.

Almost Always / Almost Never
We **almost always** bring our lunches. We **almost never** eat in a restaurant.

Frequently, Often / Seldom, Rarely
I **frequently**/**often** go out on weekends. I **seldom**/**rarely** stay home on weekends.

Using *Ever*

3A *Ever* means "at any time." We use *ever* in negative statements and in *Yes/No* questions. We also use *ever* in certain affirmative statements, for example, with *hardly*.

I **don't ever** work on weekends.
Do you **ever** go fishing?
We **hardly ever** walk to work.

3B We can use an adverb of frequency to answer a question with *Do you ever . . . ?*, but it is not necessary.

A: Do you **ever** study until midnight?
B: Yes, I do. OR I **sometimes** do.

C1 Listening for Meaning and Use
▶ Notes 1A–3A

Listen to Mark and Erica's conversation. Check (✓) the correct column.

	Mark	Erica
1. looks at diagrams	_____	✓
2. follows instructions well	_____	_____
3. doesn't usually make things	_____	_____
4. frequently cooks	_____	_____
5. rarely collects recipes	_____	_____
6. usually fixes things.	_____	_____

A. Take this magazine quiz. Check (✓) the adverb of frequency that best describes your health habits.

How Healthy Are You?

DO YOU EVER...	ALWAYS	USUALLY	SOMETIMES	RARELY	NEVER
1. take vitamins?					
2. sleep eight hours a night?					
3. eat junk food or sweets?					
4. run or swim for twenty minutes?					
5. eat green vegetables?					
6. play sports?					
7. drink eight glasses of water a day?					
8. eat fast food?					

B. Work with a partner. Take turns asking and answering the questions in part A.

A: Do you ever take vitamins?
B: Yes. Sometimes I do. OR *No. I never do.*

C3 **Expressing Opposites** ▶ Note 2

These sentences are false. Make each sentence true by using the opposite adverb of frequency. More than one answer may be possible.

1. Cats hardly ever have more than one kitten.

   <u>Cats frequently have more than one kitten.</u>

2. It seldom rains in tropical areas of the world.

   _____

3. People often live for more than 100 years.

   _____

4. It is almost always hot in Canada in October.

   _____

Vocabulary Notes

How Often . . . ? and Frequency Expressions

Use *How often . . . ?* to ask about frequency. We often use frequency expressions to answer questions with *How often . . . ?*

every day/night/afternoon/Saturday	twice a year/week
once a day/week/month/year	three times a day/month

A: **How often** do you exercise?

B: (I exercise) **every day.**

A: **How often** do you clean your apartment?

B: (I clean my apartment) **once a week.**

C4 Asking Questions About Frequency

A. Work with a partner. Take turns asking and answering questions about the things on the list. Ask questions with *How often . . . ?* Answer with frequency expressions. Take notes on your partner's responses.

1. have lunch with your friends

   A: How often do you have lunch with your friends?
   B: Every Saturday.

2. go to a nightclub

3. talk on your cell phone

4. go to a bookstore

5. study in the library

6. visit your family

7. take a bus

8. do your laundry

B. Now tell the class about your partner.

Luisa has lunch with her friends every Saturday.

A. Rewrite each sentence with a different adverb of frequency. Do not change the meaning of the sentence. More than one answer may be possible.

1. Alan isn't usually friendly.

   Alan is rarely friendly. ᴏʀ Alan isn't often friendly.

2. His co-workers don't ever ask him to go to lunch.

   _____

3. He rarely talks to people in the office.

   _____

4. Alan doesn't usually help people.

   _____

5. Alan seldom remembers his co-workers' birthdays.

   _____

6. Alan's boss likes his work all the time.

   _____

7. Alan frequently cancels his vacation.

   _____

8. Alan gets a big raise every year.

   _____

B. Write five pairs of sentences about yourself. In the first sentence, use an adverb of frequency to say how often you do something. In the second sentence, use a more specific frequency expression to explain the first sentence.

I exercise frequently.
I go to the gym three times a week.

D Combining Form, Meaning, and Use

D1 Thinking About Meaning and Use

Complete each conversation. Then discuss your answers in small groups.

1. **A:** Jack always does his homework on time.

   B: Yes. _____
   - **a.** He's a good student. *(circled)*
   - **b.** He rarely studies.
   - **c.** He seldom works hard.

2. **A:** Does it ever rain in Oman?

   B: _____
   - **a.** No, they don't.
   - **b.** Hardly ever.
   - **c.** Yes, it is.

3. **A:** Jenny is rarely home on Saturday night.

   B: _____
   - **a.** Where does she go?
   - **b.** She never goes out.
   - **c.** Is she always at home?

4. **A:** I'm frequently late for work.

   B: _____
   - **a.** Do you need a new alarm clock?
   - **b.** Does this happen often?
   - **c.** Are you ever late?

5. **A:** Do you often take vacations?

   B: No. _____
   - **a.** We sometimes do.
   - **b.** We rarely do.
   - **c.** We always do.

6. **A:** This bus never comes on time.

   B: I know. _____
   - **a.** It's never late.
   - **b.** It's usually on time.
   - **c.** It's always late.

D2 Editing

Some of these sentences have errors. Find the errors and correct them.

1. ~~Always~~ Lisa is *always* late.

2. He gets up rarely on time.

3. She seldom hears her alarm clock.

4. How often you call home?

5. I don't never study at night.

6. You always aren't on time.

7. Do you walk usually to work?

8. They almost always at home.

Beyond the Classroom

Searching for Authentic Examples

Look for a survey in an English-language newspaper or magazine, or on the Internet. Share the survey with your class. Use adverbs of frequency to report the results of the survey to the class.

Writing

Follow the steps below to write a paragraph about your own learning style.

1. Use these questions to make notes.
   - What type of learner are you?
   - What things do you find easy or difficult?
   - What types of learning do you enjoy?
   - What do you do to remember things?

2. Write a first draft. Use adverbs of frequency.

3. Read your work carefully and circle grammar, spelling, and punctuation errors. Work with a partner to decide how to fix the errors and improve the content.

4. Rewrite your draft.

   I learn from pictures and diagrams. I often draw diagrams in my notebook. The diagrams usually help me remember the lesson.

The Past

The Simple Past of *Be*

A | The Temples of Egypt

A1 | Before You Read

Discuss these questions.

What do you know about the history and culture of ancient Egypt? Who were the pharaohs? What were the pyramids?

A2 | Read

Read this excerpt from a history textbook. What was the difference between a temple and a pyramid?

THE TEMPLES OF EGYPT

The ancient Egyptians <u>were</u> great builders. Their temples and pyramids still stand today, and thousands of people visit them every year. However, 5 in ancient Egypt, the temples and pyramids (were not) for ordinary people. The pyramids were tombs for the pharaohs, the kings of ancient Egypt. The Egyptian temples were 10 very special places, too. But an Egyptian temple (was not) a tomb. For the ancient Egyptians, a temple <u>was</u> the home of a god.

The six parts of a temple were the 15 gate, the courtyard, the first hall, the second hall, the sanctuary, and the sacred lake.

The **gate** was the entrance at the front of the temple.

20 The **courtyard** was a large open room with no roof. Many pictures of

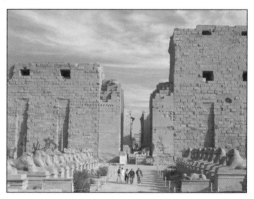

The Luxor Temple

the pharaoh and the gods were on the walls of the courtyard. The temple courtyard was open to ordinary 25 people only on special days.

The **first hall** was a large, dark room. It was light only in the center aisle. This hall was full of columns in the shape of water plants.

Floorplan of an Egyptian temple

30   The **second hall** was full of columns, too. It was very dark. It was open only to priests and the pharaoh.

    The **sanctuary** was the most special and important part of the temple. It 35 was a dark and mysterious place. Like the second hall, this room was open only to priests and the pharaoh. A statue of the god was in the middle of the sanctuary.

40   The **sacred lake** was a pool of water next to the temple. The water from the sacred lake was important for special rituals.

---

god: a being that people worship
priest: a religious leader
ritual: a ceremony

sacred: holy
temple: a religious place
tomb: a place for a dead body

A3   After You Read

Match each part of the temple with its description.

_d_ **1.** gate

a. a special room with a statue of a god

_____ **2.** courtyard

b. a pool of holy water outside the temple

_____ **3.** first hall

c. an open room with pictures of the pharaoh

_____ **4.** second hall

d. an entrance at the front of the temple

_____ **5.** sanctuary

e. a dark room with light in the center aisle

_____ **6.** sacred lake

f. a very dark room open only to priests and the pharaoh

B The Simple Past of *Be*

Examining Form

Look back at the excerpt on pages 170–171 and complete the tasks below. Then discuss your answers and read the Form charts to check them.

1. Look at the underlined examples of *be* in the simple past. Are they affirmative forms or negative forms? What are their subjects?

2. Look at the circled examples of *be* in the simple past. Are they affirmative forms or negative forms? Does the word *not* come before or after the verb?

3. Find four more affirmative examples of the simple past of *be*.

Affirmative Statements		
SUBJECT	**WAS/WERE**	
I	**was**	
You	**were**	
He She It	**was**	helpful.
We		
You	**were**	
They		

Negative Statements		
SUBJECT	**WAS/WERE + NOT**	
I	**was not** **wasn't**	
You	**were not** **weren't**	
He She It	**was not** **wasn't**	helpful.
We		
You	**were not** **weren't**	
They		

Yes/No Questions

WAS/WERE	SUBJECT	
Was	I	
Were	you	
Was	he she it	helpful?
Were	we you they	

Short Answers

YES	SUBJECT	WAS/WERE	NO	SUBJECT	WAS/WERE + NOT
	you	**were.**		you	**weren't.**
	I	**was.**		I	**wasn't.**
Yes,	he she it	**was.**	**No,**	he she it	**wasn't.**
	you			you	
	we	**were.**		we	**weren't.**
	they			they	

Information Questions

WH- WORD	WAS/WERE	SUBJECT	
Where	**was**	he	last week?
Why	**were**	you	in Hawaii?
What	**was**	that noise?	
When	**were**	we	in Boston?
Who		you	with?
How		the desserts?	

WH- WORD (SUBJECT)	WAS		
Who	**was**		in Rome?
What			in the car?

Answers

He **was** in London.
For Tom's wedding.
It was a barking dog.
In 1995.
My brother.
They **were** delicious!

We **were.**
My purse.

- The verb *be* has two past forms: *was* and *were*.
- In negative statements and negative short answers, combine *was* and *were* with *not* to make the contractions *wasn't* and *weren't*.

Listening for Form

🎧 Listen to each sentence. What verb form do you hear? Check (✓) the correct column.

	WAS	WASN'T	WERE	WEREN'T
1.	✓			
2.				
3.				
4.				
5.				
6.				
7.				
8.				

B2 **Working on Affirmative Statements**

Complete the paragraph with *was* or *were*.

Alexander the Great (356–323 B.C.)

____was____ a great Greek military leader.
    1

His birthplace _____ Pella, the ancient
              2

capital of Macedonia. Alexander's parents

_____ Philip II, king of Macedonia,
    3

and Olympias, a princess of Epirus. His

teacher _____ the philosopher
        4

Aristotle. As a king and general, Alexander

_____ very popular with his soldiers.
    5

They _____ very loyal to him. By
     6

Alexander the Great

323 B.C., countries from Turkey to Afghanistan _____ under his control. At
                                               7

the time of his death, Alexander _____ only 33 years old.
                                 8

The facts below are false. Correct each one by rewriting it as a negative statement.
Then use the word or phrase in parentheses to write a true affirmative statement.

1. The pharaohs were generals. (kings)

   The pharaohs weren't generals. They were kings.

2. Cleopatra was a Persian general. (Egyptian queen)

   _____

3. Columbus was a lawyer. (explorer)

   _____

4. Picasso and Rembrandt were astronomers. (artists)

   _____

5. William Shakespeare was a French writer. (English)

   _____

6. Cervantes was an American inventor. (Spanish writer)

   _____

7. Marie Curie and Albert Einstein were doctors. (scientists)

   _____

8. Beethoven was a German king. (composer)

   _____

A. Form *Yes/No* questions. Use the words and phrases. Punctuate your sentences correctly.

1. an only child *Were you an only child?*

2. a good student _____

3. your mother/a housewife _____

4. your hometown/large _____

5. your teachers/friendly _____

6. your home/near a beach _____

B. Work with a partner. Take turns asking and answering the questions in part A.

A: Were you an only child?
B: No, I wasn't.

B5 Forming Information Questions

A. Form information questions. Use the words and phrases. Punctuate your sentences correctly.

1. What/Persia *What was Persia?*

2. Who/Alexander the Great _____

3. When/the American Revolution _____

4. Where/the Mongols from _____

5. Who/Marie Curie and Albert Einstein _____

6. What/the pyramids _____

B. Answer the questions in part A in your notebook. Use the words and phrases.

1. the old name of Iran

   Persia was the old name of Iran.

2. a Greek military leader

3. in the eighteenth century

4. Mongolia

5. famous scientists

6. the tombs of pharaohs

The Simple Past of *Be*

Examining Meaning and Use

Read the sentences and answer the questions below. Then discuss your answers and read the Meaning and Use Notes to check them.

a. My uncle was a doctor.

b. The weather is rainy.

c. Yesterday the children were happy.

d. Twenty years ago he was a great athlete.

e. They weren't in Brazil last year.

f. Shakespeare was from England.

1. Which sentences show situations that existed in the past? Which show situations that exist in the present?

2. Which sentences use a word or phrase that tells you exactly when a situation existed in the past? Underline the word or phrase in each sentence.

Meaning and Use Notes

> ### Common Uses of *Be* in the Simple Past
>
> **1** Use the simple past of *be* to talk about people, things, or situations that existed in the past.
>
> *Conditions*
> John and Sandra **were** sick yesterday.
> Keisha **was** hungry.
>
> *Physical Characteristics*
> Last year Soon-jin's hair **was** long.
> The school **was** small.
>
> *Occupations*
> Her brother **was** a taxi driver for four years.
>
> *Location and Origin*
> Those two new students **were** here yesterday.
> Alexander the Great **was** from Macedonia.

(Continued on page 178)

2 When we use the simple past of *be*, we often use a past time expression like *yesterday, last night/week/month*. We also use a period of time + *ago*. These past time expressions can occur at the beginning or end of a sentence.

I wasn't in school **yesterday.**	**The day before yesterday** was Monday.
Last night they were at a party.	**Last month** we were in Argentina.
Irina's birthday was **ten days ago.**	**Five minutes ago** Mike was in the kitchen.

C1 Listening for Meaning and Use
▶ Note 1

🎧 Listen to each sentence. Is it about the past or the present? Check (✓) the correct column.

	PAST	PRESENT
1.	✓	
2.		
3.		
4.		
5.		
6.		

C2 Using Past Time Expressions with *Was/Were*
▶ Note 2

Complete each sentence. Use *was/wasn't* or *were/weren't* to make true statements.

1. I ___wasn't___ at home last night.

2. My friends _____ in school yesterday.

3. My best friend _____ in New Orleans three days ago.

4. I _____ happy about the grades on my last test.

5. Our teacher _____ in class the day before yesterday.

6. The movie *Casablanca* _____ on TV last night.

Vocabulary Notes

Was Born and *Were Born*

When we talk about the birth of a person, we use *was born* and *were born*.

Alexander the Great **was born** in Macedonia.

The twins **were born** in 1978.

Use these questions to ask about a birthplace or birthday.

When **was** he **born**?	**Was** Alexander **born** in Macedonia?
Where **were** they **born**?	**Were** Ana and Rosa **born** in Uruguay?

C3 Guessing Where and When People Were Born

A. Guess where and when these famous people were born. Use the places and dates below to fill in the chart.

Places: China Egypt England Germany Holland Italy Poland Spain

Dates: 551 B.C. 69 B.C. 1451 1564 1606 1867 1879 1881

		PLACE OF BIRTH	YEAR OF BIRTH
1.	Cleopatra	Egypt	69 B.C.
2.	Columbus		
3.	Confucius		
4.	Marie Curie		
5.	Einstein		
6.	Picasso		
7.	Rembrandt		
8.	Shakespeare		

B. Work with a partner. Take turns asking and answering questions about the people in the chart.

A: Where was Cleopatra born?
B: That's easy. She was born in Egypt. When was she born?
A: Hmm . . . . In 69 B.C.?
B: I don't know. Let's see.

C. Now see Appendix 12 to check your answers. How many correct answers do you have?

C4) Guessing About the Past ► Note 1

Work with a partner. Think of a famous person from the past. Do not tell your partner the person's name. Take turns asking *Yes/No* questions about your partner's famous person. Try to guess the person's name.

A: *Was this person a man?*
B: *Yes, he was.*

A: *Was he an astronaut?*
B: *No, he wasn't.*

A: *Was he a scientist?*
B: *Yes, he was.*

A: *Is it Albert Einstein?*
B: *Yes, it is!*

C5) Talking About Your Past ► Notes 1, 2

A. Work with a partner. Take turns asking and answering the following questions about your lives. Make notes about your partner's answers.

1. Where were you ten years ago?

2. Were you a student? If not, what were you?

3. What were you like?

4. What were your hobbies?

5. Who were your best friends?

6. What were your best friends like?

B. Change partners. Tell your new partner about your first partner. Use your notes.

Ten years ago Yuji was in Japan. He was a student in the sixth grade of elementary school. He was a good athlete...

C6) Describing Places in the Past ► Note 1

A. What do you remember about your first school? Answer the questions.

1. Where was your first school?

2. How long were you a student there?

3. What was the school like?

4. Who was your favorite teacher?

5. What were your favorite lessons?

6. Were you a good student?

B. Write a paragraph describing your school. Use your answers in part A to guide you.

My first school was in Bogotá. I was a student there for six years. It was an old school with very big classrooms. My favorite teacher was Mr. Lopez. My favorite lessons were math, geography, and science. I was a good student.

D Combining Form, Meaning, and Use

D1 Thinking About Meaning and Use

Complete each conversation. Then discuss your answers in small groups.

1. **A:** _____

   B: No. It was very small.
   - **a.** Where do you live?
   - **(b.)** Was your house big?
   - **c.** Who was in your house?

2. **A:** When were you born?

   B: _____
   - **a.** Last night.
   - **b.** Twenty years ago.
   - **c.** In Tokyo.

3. **A:** What was the weather like in Miami?

   B: _____
   - **a.** It was hot and rainy.
   - **b.** It is cold.
   - **c.** It rains.

4. **A:** Who was at the party?

   B: I don't know. _____
   - **a.** I wasn't there.
   - **b.** I am not there.
   - **c.** I'm there.

5. **A:** _____

   B: In South America.
   - **a.** When was your father born?
   - **b.** Where was your grandmother born?
   - **c.** What was your grandfather?

6. **A:** Marta's hair is very long.

   B: That's impossible! _____
   - **a.** It was long yesterday.
   - **b.** It was short last week.
   - **c.** Marta's hair was dark.

7. **A:** _____

   B: The bus was late.
   - **a.** When weren't you on time?
   - **b.** Why weren't you on time?
   - **c.** When were you on time?

8. **A:** Was Confucius a Chinese general?

   B: _____. He was a Chinese philosopher.
   - **a.** No, he wasn't.
   - **b.** Yes, he was.
   - **c.** I think so.

Find the errors in this paragraph and correct them.

was

My best friend in elementary school is Hanna. We was very close friends. Hanna born in Seoul in 1984. Her parents was teachers, and they very kind people. Their house was very beautiful. Her grandparents were also very kind, but they're very old. Hanna's little brother was very funny. His toys always on the living-room floor and his dog always with him. He not naughty like my little brother.

▶ Beyond the Classroom

Searching for Authentic Examples

Look in an English-language book or on the Internet for information about a person from the past. Find three examples of the past of *be*. Write them in your notebook and share them with your class.

Writing

Follow the steps below to write a paragraph about a famous person from the past.

1. Do research in the library or on the Internet. Use these questions to make notes.
   - What was this person's job or profession?
   - When was this person born?
   - What was this person like?
   - Why was this person famous or important?

2. Write a first draft. Use the simple past of *be*.

3. Read your work carefully and circle grammar, spelling, and punctuation errors. Work with a partner to decide how to fix the errors and improve the content.

4. Rewrite your draft.

    Confucius was a Chinese philosopher. He was born in the ancient province of Lu in about 551 B.C. . . .

The Simple Past

Fashions in History

A1 Before You Read

Discuss these questions.

What are some of today's fashions? Do you like them? Why or why not? What do you know about fashions of the past?

A2 Read

Read the excerpt from a history textbook on the following page. What were some of the fashions in the eighteenth century and the nineteenth century?

A3 After You Read

Look at the chart. Is the fashion from the eighteenth century or the nineteenth century? Check (✓) the correct column.

	FASHION	EIGHTEENTH CENTURY (1700s)	NINETEENTH CENTURY (1800s)
1.	pale skin		✓
2.	gloves		
3.	elaborate hairstyles		
4.	high boots		
5.	heavy clothing		
6.	powdered wigs		

FASHIONS *in* HISTORY

Fashions are always changing. The fashions of past centuries often seem strange or funny to us. In the United States and Europe, for example, upper-class men and women of the
5 1700s wore white wigs. The wigs were white because people <u>covered</u> them with white powder. Wealthy women in France in the 1770s did something even stranger. They made a paste of flour and water. Then they
10 put it on their hair to make elaborate hairstyles. They often added feathers, lace, and ribbons. Some women even <u>placed</u> vases of real flowers and small birdcages with live birds in their hair.

French hairstyle from the 1770s

People often ask this question: Why did Napoleon Bonaparte keep one hand inside
15 his coat? Certainly, it was not because he did not have gloves. He actually owned 300 pairs! In the nineteenth century, many wealthy people wore gloves indoors and outdoors. Gloves became popular because they protected the hands and helped keep them soft. Soft hands showed that
20 a person was rich and did not need to work.

In the nineteenth century, life was not easy for fashionable European women. They wore about 30 pounds of clothing. This often included a long dress of heavy material, several undergarments,
25 a big hat with flowers or feathers, a veil, and high boots. Each piece of clothing had a purpose. For example, they wore high boots because women needed to cover their legs down to the ankle. They never went out without a hat because
30 they wanted to have pale skin—another sign of wealth. For this reason, women also put white powder on their faces.

European nineteenth-century dress

---

ankle: area where the foot connects to the leg
elaborate: complicated, detailed
lace: loosely knit material with beautiful patterns

ribbons: long, thin pieces of material
undergarments: clothing worn under another piece of clothing
veil: a net used to cover the face

B Simple Past Statements

Examining Form

Look back at the excerpt on page 185 and complete the tasks below. Then discuss your answers and read the Form charts to check them.

1. Look at the underlined examples of regular verbs in the simple past. What ending do we add to the base form of regular verbs ending in *-e*?

2. What ending do we add to the base form of all other regular verbs?

3. Look at the irregular verbs below and their irregular simple past forms. Do the simple past forms have a common ending?

   wear — wore   do — did   make — made   put — put

4. Look at the circled example of a negative form in the simple past. Find one more example of this form. How many parts does the negative form have? What are they?

REGULAR VERBS

Affirmative Statements		
SUBJECT	BASE FORM OF VERB + *-D/-ED*	
I		
You		
He She It	**arrived worked**	yesterday.
We		
You		
They		

Negative Statements			
SUBJECT	*DID + NOT*	BASE FORM OF VERB	
I			
You			
He She It	**did not didn't**	**arrive work**	yesterday.
We			
You			
They			

Affirmative Statements

SUBJECT	SIMPLE PAST FORM	
I		
You		
He She It	left went won	yesterday.
We		
You		
They		

Negative Statements

SUBJECT	DID + NOT	BASE FORM OF VERB	
I			
You			
He She It	did not didn't	leave go win	yesterday.
We			
You			
They			

Regular Verbs

• To form the simple past of most regular verbs, add -ed to the base form.

  work — work**ed**   cover — cover**ed**

• If the base form of a regular verb ends in -e, add -d.

  arrive — arrive**d**   place — place**d**

• See Appendix 6 for spelling rules for verbs ending in -ed.

Irregular Verbs

• Some verbs are irregular in the simple past tense. These are some common examples.

  BASE FORM — SIMPLE PAST

become — became	go — went	say — said
buy — bought	have — had	see — saw
come — came	hear — heard	spend — spent
do — did	keep — kept	speak — spoke
drive — drove	know — knew	take — took
eat — ate	leave — left	wake — woke
find — found	make — made	wear — wore
forget — forgot	meet — met	win — won
give — gave	put — put	write — wrote

• See Appendix 8 for irregular verbs and their simple past forms.

Negative Forms

• To form a negative statement in the simple past with a regular or irregular verb, use the base form of the verb after *did + not.*

🎧 Listen for the verb in each sentence. Is the verb in the simple past or the simple present? Choose the form you hear.

1. **a.** lives
   b. lived *(circled)*

2. **a.** call
   b. called

3. **a.** wear
   b. wore

4. **a.** think
   b. thought

5. **a.** play
   b. played

6. **a.** cover
   b. covered

7. **a.** seems
   b. seemed

8. **a.** is
   b. was

B2 Working on Regular Simple Past Verbs

Complete the paragraph. Use the simple past form of each verb in parentheses.

A strange thing _happened_
        1
(happen) at our salon today. At about 10:00,

the door _____ (open) and a young
                2

man _____ (walk) in. He said he
              3

_____ (not want) a normal haircut.
        4

He _____ (want) a new hairstyle.
           5

He _____ (ask) me to cut only one
             6

side! I _____ (lift) my scissors and
              7

_____ (start) cutting. I _____
        8   9

(finish) one side, and I _____ (stop). He _____ (look) in the mirror and
                                    10   11

_____ (smile). "It's perfect!" he _____ (exclaim). Then he _____
        12   13   14

(hand) me $10 and said happily, "A normal haircut is $20, so $10 should be fine!"

Complete the letter. Use the simple past form of each verb in parentheses.

Dear Marta,

I __had__ (have) a great time in Washington, D.C. The plane tickets
1

were very inexpensive, so I _____ (buy) two and _____ (take)
2   3

my friend Val with me. We _____ (go) to a lot of museums. In fact,
4

we _____ (spend) one day at the National Museum of American
5

History. We _____ (see) a really interesting exhibit on clothes of the
6

past. People _____ (wear) some very strange clothes in the old
7

days! We _____ (eat) very well, too! We _____ (find) a different
8   9

restaurant every night. We also _____ (meet) a lot of interesting
10

people. Write soon and tell me about San Francisco.

B4 **Contrasting Negative and Affirmative Simple Past Statements**

The statements below are false. Make each one true by changing it to a negative
statement. Then write a true affirmative statement. Use the words in parentheses
in place of the underlined words. Write in your notebook.

1. Nineteenth-century women wore <u>short dresses</u>. (long dresses)

   Nineteenth-century women didn't wear short dresses. They wore long dresses.

2. In the 1700s upper-class men and women covered their wigs with <u>black</u> powder. (white)

3. In the 1700s aristocratic French women had <u>simple hairstyles</u>. (elaborate hairstyles)

4. French women used <u>hairspray</u> on their hair. (paste)

5. Napoleon owned hundreds of <u>hats</u>. (gloves)

Pronunciation Notes

Pronunciation of Verbs Ending in *-ed*

The final *-ed* of regular simple past verbs has three pronunciations: /t/, /d/, and /ɪd/. The pronunciation depends on the final sound of the base form of the verb.

1. If the base form of the verb ends with the sounds /p/, /k/, /tʃ/, /f/, /s/, /ʃ/, or /ks/, then we pronounce the final *-ed* as /t/.

laugh – laughed /læft/	slice – sliced /slaɪst/
look – looked /lʊkt/	fix – fixed /fɪkst/

2. If the base form ends with a vowel sound or the sounds /b/, /g/, /dʒ/, /v/, /ð/, /z/, /ʒ/, /m/, /n/, /ŋ/, /l/, or /r/, then we pronounce the final *-ed* as /d/.

try – tried /traɪd/	shave – shaved /sheɪvd/
bang – banged /bæŋd/	rain – rained /reɪnd/

3. If the base form of the verb ends with the sound /d/ or /t/, then we pronounce the final *-ed* as /ɪd/. This adds an extra syllable to the word.

need – needed /ˈnidɪd/	start – started /ˈstartɪd/
decide – decided /dɪˈsaɪdɪd/	wait – waited /ˈweɪtɪd/

B5) Pronouncing Final *-ed*

A. 🎧 Look at the chart. Listen for each verb alone and in a sentence. What final sound do you hear? Check (✓) the correct column.

		/t/	/d/	/ɪd/
1.	needed			✓
2.	stopped			
3.	waited			
4.	knocked			
5.	gained			
6.	borrowed			
7.	helped			
8.	hated			

B. Work with a partner. Take turns saying each of the word pairs. Choose the correct pronunciation for each *-ed* ending.

1. try – tried   /t/ (/d/) /ɪd/

2. laugh – laughed   /t/   /d/   /ɪd/

3. rain – rained   /t/   /d/   /ɪd/

4. invite – invited   /t/   /d/   /ɪd/

5. fail – failed   /t/   /d/   /ɪd/

6. hike – hiked   /t/   /d/   /ɪd/

7. wash – washed   /t/   /d/   /ɪd/

8. want – wanted   /t/   /d/   /ɪd/

B6) Changing the Simple Present to the Simple Past

A. Change the verbs in the paragraph from the simple present to the simple past. Rewrite the paragraph in your notebook.

Teresa wakes up at 7:00 and takes a shower. Then she dries her hair and brushes her teeth. She cooks a light breakfast and drinks a cup of coffee. She waits for her friend Eva on the corner, and they walk to the office together. On the way, they discuss their jobs and plan their day. At 8:45 they arrive at the office and start their day. Teresa works hard all day, and after work, she exercises and lifts weights at the gym. She gets home at 7:00 and prepares a simple meal. After dinner, she relaxes and listens to music. Then she watches the evening news and goes to bed.

Teresa woke up at 7:00 and took a shower. Then she . . .

B. Work with a partner. Find the past tense verbs in your paragraph in part A. Write them in the correct column.

REGULAR PAST TENSE FORMS			IRREGULAR PAST TENSE FORMS
/t/	/d/	/ɪd/	
			woke up

C. With your partner, take turns reading the paragraph you wrote in part A.

C **Simple Past Questions**

Examining Form

Read the sentences and answer the questions below. Then discuss your answers and read the Form charts to check them.

1a. Do you eat breakfast?　　**2a.** When does the class start?
1b. Did you eat breakfast?　　**2b.** When did the class start?

1. Which questions are in the simple past? How do you know?

2. Which is a *Yes/No* question in the simple past? What word comes before the subject? What form of the verb follows the subject?

3. Which is an information question in the simple past? What word comes between the *wh-* word and the subject? What form of the verb follows the subject?

Yes/No Questions			
DID	**SUBJECT**	**BASE FORM OF VERB**	
Did	I		
	you		
	he she it	**arrive leave**	yesterday?
	we		
	you		
	they		

Short Answers						
YES	**SUBJECT**	**DID**	**NO**	**SUBJECT**	**DID + NOT**	
Yes,	I	**did.**	**No,**	I	**didn't.**	
	you			you		
	he she it			he she it		
	you			you		
	we			we		
	they			they		

Information Questions					Answers
WH- WORD	**DID**	**SUBJECT**	**BASE FORM OF VERB**		
Who		I	**meet**	at dinner?	Your friend Jane.
What		you	**have**	for breakfast?	I **had** cereal.
Where	**did**	he	**go**	last night?	To Steve's house.
When		we	**call**	them?	You **called** them last week.
Why		you	**study**	so late?	Because we **had** a big test.
How		they	**enjoy**	the film?	They **loved** it.

WH- WORD (SUBJECT)			SIMPLE PAST FORM		
Who			**left**	yesterday?	Pete.
What			**arrived**	in the mail?	A letter.

- Use *did* to form most questions in the simple past.
- Use the base form of the verb after the subject in most simple past questions. Do not use a simple past form.

    Who did Gloria **call**?   Did Alex **see** you?

⚠️ Do not use *did* in information questions when *who* or *what* is the subject.

    What **happened** last night?   Who **left** early?

C1 **Listening for Form**

🎧 Listen to each sentence. Check (✓) the form of *do* that you hear. For sentences with no form of *do*, check (✓) the last column (Ø).

	DO	DOES	DID	Ø
1.			✓	
2.				
3.				
4.				
5.				
6.				

A. Form simple past questions in your notebook. Use the words and phrases. Then look at the pictures and answer your questions with short answers. If an answer is *no*, write a true statement. Punctuate your sentences correctly.

1. Carl and Rosa/go to the bank

Did Carl and Rosa go to the bank?
No. They went to the mall.

4. they/eat/hamburgers for lunch

2. Carl/buy/a shirt

5. they/look/at dolls

3. Rosa/go to the hairdresser's

6. they/meet/their friends

B. Work with a partner. Take turns asking and answering the questions in part A.

C. Now write six *Yes/No* questions to find out about your partner's activities yesterday. Take turns asking and answering each other's questions.

A: Did you wake up early yesterday?
B: No, I didn't. I woke up at 11:00.

C3 Working on Information Questions

Write information questions about the underlined words or phrases in each statement.

1. Carol studied art <u>in Paris.</u>

   Where did Carol study art?

2. Carol made <u>her own clothes</u>.

   _____

3. Carol graduated from college <u>in 1999</u>.

   _____

4. <u>Carol</u> worked for a fashion designer.

   _____

5. <u>Her boss</u> taught her the latest fashions.

   _____

6. <u>The fashion designer</u> loved Carol's work.

   _____

7. Carol photographed <u>her designs</u>.

   _____

8. Carol won a prize <u>in 2001</u>.

   _____

Informally Speaking

Spoken Forms of *Did* + Pronoun

🎧 Look at the cartoon and listen to the sentence. How is the underlined form in the cartoon different from what you hear?

> Josh! What <u>did you</u> do to my new floor?

We often use the spoken form of *did you* /ˈdɪdʒə/ and *did he* /ˈdɪdi/ in conversation.

STANDARD FORM	WHAT YOU MIGHT HEAR
Did you go yesterday?	"/ˈdɪdʒə/ go yesterday?"
Did he leave early?	"/ˈdɪdi/ leave early?"
Where **did you** study?	"Where /ˈdɪdʒə/ study?"

C4 Understanding Informal Speech

🎧 Listen to the conversation. Write the standard form of the words you hear.

1. **A:** _Did he_ come home late last night?

   B: Yes. He got in at 9:00.

2. **A:** What time _____ call him?

   B: About 10:00.

3. **A:** How _____ get home from the airport?

   B: He took a taxi.

4. **A:** _____ have a good time in Hawaii?

   B: Yes. He loved it!

5. **A:** _____ invite him for dinner on Friday?

   B: Yes I did.

The Simple Past

Examining Meaning and Use

Read the sentences and answer the questions below. Then discuss your answers and read the Meaning and Use Notes to check them.

    a. David works in Seattle.
    b. David worked in Seattle for a long time.

1. Which sentence shows that David has a job in Seattle now?

2. Which sentence shows that David does not have a job in Seattle now?

Meaning and Use Notes

Past Actions and States

1A Use the simple past for actions that started and finished in the past. The actions can be from the recent past (a short time ago) or from the distant past (a long time ago).

Recent Past

She **washed** her hair <u>this morning</u>.

Distant Past

The war **started** <u>in 1776</u>.

1B Use the simple past for states that were true in the past.

Recent Past

She **was** sick <u>this morning</u>.

Distant Past

Gloves **were** popular <u>in the nineteenth century</u>.

Past Time Expressions

2 As with the simple past of *be*, we often use past time expressions with verbs in the simple past to say when an action happened. Past time expressions can come at the beginning or at the end of the sentence.

They went to Japan **last week**.
He left **ten minutes ago**.
We stayed **for three hours**.

Last night we saw a great movie.
Two years ago I went to Mexico.
I was ill **yesterday**.

Listen to each sentence. Is the action or state in the past or present? Check (✓) the correct column.

	PAST	PRESENT
1.	✓	
2.		
3.		
4.		
5.		
6.		
7.		
8.		

D2 Referring to Past Time Expressions ► Notes 1A, 2

A. In your notebook, write questions with *when* in the simple past. Use the words and phrases. Then write a true answer to the questions. Use past time expressions. Punctuate your sentences correctly.

1. take/vacation

   When did you take a vacation?
   I took a vacation last month.

2. see/your friends

3. go/the movies

4. eat/pizza

5. take/a test

6. finish/high school

B. Write five more simple past questions with *when*.

   When did you have your first English class?

C. Work with a partner. Take turns asking and answering each other's questions in part B. Use a time expression in each answer.

   A: When did you have your first English class?
   B: I had my first English class two years ago.

Beyond the Sentence

Connecting Ideas in the Simple Past

We can use sequence words such as *first*, *next*, *then*, and *later* with time expressions to help connect ideas in a story. Time expressions help us place events at **specific** times in the past. They also help us show the passage of time.

> **Five years ago** Derek met a beautiful woman at a party. **The next day** he saw her again at the library. **Later that evening** he called her and asked her out. They had their first date **two days later**. **The next week** they spent every day together. **A year later** they announced their engagement.

D3 Connecting Events in the Past

Look at the pictures. Write a paragraph in your notebook to describe Amy's bad day. Use the time expressions and sequence words. Begin with:

Last week Amy had a really bad day. First, she got up late. Then, . . .

1. get up late

3. drop the coffee pot

5. arrive at work / see a sign on the door

2. burn her shirt

4. miss the bus

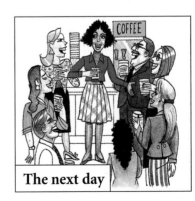

6. tell the story at work / they laugh

D4 Writing About Events in the Past

► Notes 1A, 1B, 2

A. Think about a bad day you had. In your notebook, write a list of at least five events that happened.

I didn't hear my alarm clock.

B. Now write a paragraph. Connect the events with sequence words and past time expressions. Start with a sentence that tells when the events happened.

Last Monday I had a really bad day. First, I didn't hear my alarm clock, and I got to English class 20 minutes late. . . .

D5 Talking About the Past

► Notes 1A, 1B, 2

A. Work with a small group. Write questions about life one hundred years ago. Write a question for each topic.

	TOPIC	QUESTION
1.	transportation	How did people travel?
2.	jobs	
3.	school	
4.	food	
5.	clothes	
6.	families	
7.	communication	
8.	entertainment	

B. Take turns asking and answering the questions in part A. Offer as many different answers to each question as possible.

A: How did people travel?
B: People traveled by horse and cart.
C: They also traveled on foot.

Combining Form, Meaning, and Use

E1 Thinking About Meaning and Use

Complete each conversation. Then discuss your answers in small groups.

1. **A:** _____

   B: My ten-year-old brother.

   a. Who drove you to school?

   b. Who did you drive to school?

   c. When did you go?

2. **A:** What did you do yesterday?

   B: _____

   a. My homework.

   b. Last night.

   c. Yes, I did it.

3. **A:** I missed class on Monday.

   B: _____

   a. Why did you miss him?

   b. Are you in class now?

   c. Did you wake up late?

4. **A:** What started the fire?

   B: _____

   a. A cigarette.

   b. Two weeks ago.

   c. In a restaurant.

5. **A:** _____

   B: They used horses and wagons.

   a. Where did people go?

   b. When did people travel?

   c. How did people travel?

6. **A:** _____

   B: I have no idea.

   a. Why did Victorian women wear all those clothes?

   b. Why do Victorian women wear long dresses?

   c. Do Victorian women have long hair?

7. **A:** When did you arrive?

   B: _____

   a. By train.

   b. Yesterday evening.

   c. Yes, I did

8. **A:** Who _____

   B: Tom did.

   a. did he break the window?

   b. break the window?

   c. broke the window?

Find the errors in this paragraph and correct them.

graduated
I ~~graduate~~ from high school in 1995. My high school years are very difficult. For one thing, my school were very far from my house, so I didn't went out with my friends very often. In addition, my parents didn't like my friends. They worried about me, and they always ask me lots of questions. Where you went last night? Who you with? What time did you get home? I hated all of those questions. Sometimes I didn't told the truth. To be honest, I feel bad about lying.

▶ Beyond the Classroom

Searching for Authentic Examples

Look for simple past sentences in English-language newspapers and magazines, or on the Internet. Find three regular and three irregular simple past verbs. Write the sentences in your notebook and share them with your class.

Writing

Follow the steps below to write a paragraph about life in your country one hundred years ago.

1. Use these questions to make notes.
   - Where did most people live?
   - What kind of work did most people do?
   - What kind of clothes did people wear?
   - What kind of transportation did people use?

2. Write a first draft. Use the simple past.

3. Read your work carefully and circle grammar, spelling, and punctuation errors. Work with a partner to decide how to fix the errors and improve the content.

4. Rewrite your draft.

   One hundred years ago, most Polish people lived in the countryside. They lived in small villages. . . .

The Past Continuous

A Unusual Disasters in History

A1 Before You Read

Discuss these questions.

What is a disaster? What kinds of things cause disasters? Can you think of any recent disasters?

A2 Read

Read this magazine article to find out about two unusual disasters. What were their causes?

Unusual DISASTERS in History

The Great Chicago Fire

According to legend, the worst disaster in the history of the city of Chicago began in a barn on the night of Sunday, 5 October 8, 1871. A woman named Mrs. O'Leary <u>was milking</u> her cow when the cow kicked over a lantern and started a fire. According to historians, a combination of bad planning and dry 10 weather allowed the fire to destroy the city. While firefighters <u>were fighting</u> the fire downtown, the wind blew it across the river. Suddenly, the city was burning on both sides of the river! The 15 firefighters didn't have enough men or equipment to fight the fire. Chicago was still burning when rain finally came on Tuesday and put out the fire. In the end, 2,000 acres of land and 18,000 20 buildings burned—all because of a cow. Amazingly, Mrs. O'Leary's house survived!

Boston's Sea of Molasses

January 15, 1919, was a beautiful Sunday in Boston. The sun was shining. Many
25 people were enjoying the unusually warm weather. Unfortunately, the beautiful weather caused a disaster. A huge tank with two million gallons of molasses was sitting in the hot sun at the
30 Purity Distilling Company in downtown Boston. The sun heated the molasses, the molasses expanded, and the huge tank exploded. Soon a giant wave of sticky molasses almost two stories high was
35 spreading through the streets. The river of molasses was not moving very fast, but it trapped many people in their houses. It killed 21 men, women, and children and destroyed many buildings. It took several weeks to clean up the city streets and
40 buildings. For many years after that the sweet smell of molasses filled the air on warm days.

---

barn: a building where farmers keep animals such as cows and horses

expand: become bigger

lantern: a light that you can carry, often with a flame

legend: a story that may or may not be true

molasses: a thick, dark, sticky syrup made from sugar

tank: a large container for gas or liquid

A3 **After You Read**

Write *T* for true or *F* for false for each statement. Then change the false statements to true ones.

__F__ **1.** Mrs. O'Leary started the Chicago fire.

Mrs. O'Leary's cow started the Chicago fire.

_____ **2.** The Chicago fire burned for one day.

_____ **3.** The fire destroyed 2,000 buildings.

_____ **4.** Extremely cold weather caused the explosion at the Purity Distillery Company.

_____ **5.** Twenty-one people died in the Purity Distilling Company explosion.

_____ **6.** People smelled molasses in the air for years after the disaster.

B Past Continuous

Examining Form

Look back at the article on pages 204–205 and complete the tasks below. Then discuss your answers and read the Form charts to check them.

1. Look at the two underlined examples of the affirmative form of the the past continuous. Each has two words. What are they?

2. Find two more affirmative examples of the past continuous.

3. Look at the circled example of the negative form of the past continuous. How many words does it have? What are they?

Affirmative Statements			
SUBJECT	WAS/WERE	BASE FORM OF VERB + -ING	
I	was	working	at 5:00.
You	were		
He She It	was		
We	were		
You			
They			

Negative Statements			
SUBJECT	WAS/WERE + NOT	BASE FORM OF VERB + -ING	
I	was not wasn't	working	at 5:00.
You	were not weren't		
He She It	was not wasn't		
We	were not weren't		
You			
They			

- In speaking and informal writing, we often use the contractions *wasn't* and *weren't* in negative past continuous statements.
- See Appendix 3 for spelling rules for verbs ending in *-ing*.

Yes/No Questions

WAS/ WERE	SUBJECT	BASE FORM OF VERB + -ING	
Was	I		
Were	you		
Was	he she it	**working**	at 5:00?
Were	we you they		

Short Answers

YES	SUBJECT	WAS/ WERE	NO	SUBJECT	WAS/WERE + NOT
	you	**were.**		you	**weren't.**
	I	**was.**		I	**wasn't.**
Yes,	he she it	**was.**	**No,**	he she it	**wasn't.**
	you			you	
	we	**were.**		we	**weren't.**
	they			they	

Information Questions

WH- WORD	WAS/ WERE	SUBJECT	BASE FORM OF VERB + -ING
How	**was**	I	**doing?**
What	**were**	you	
Who	**was**	he	**calling?**
Why		we	
When	**were**	you	**driving?**
Where		they	

WH- WORD (SUBJECT)	WAS		BASE FORM OF VERB + -ING
Who	**was**		**reading?**
What			**happening?**

Answers

Great.

I **was cooking** dinner.

He **was calling** David.

Because the trains **weren't running**.

Yesterday morning.

On the highway.

Marta **was reading**.

The dogs **were barking**.

⚠ When *who or what* is the subject of the question, do not use a subject pronoun.

🎧 Listen to each sentence about a fire in a building. Choose the answer you hear.

1. a. is burning
   (b.) was burning
   c. burned

2. a. are walking
   b. were walking
   c. walked

3. a. are calling
   b. were calling
   c. called

4. a. are arriving
   b. were arriving
   c. arrived

5. a. is burning
   b. was burning
   c. burned

6. a. is working
   b. was working
   c. worked

B2) Forming Affirmative and Negative Past Continuous Statements

Form an affirmative and a negative statement about what Jack and his friends were and were not doing at 9:00 P.M. yesterday evening. Use the words and phrases. Punctuate your sentences correctly.

1. Jack/watch/TV/not do/his homework

   Jack was watching TV. He wasn't doing his homework.

2. Marta and Derek/play/chess/not watch/TV

   _____

3. Jenny/study/for a history test/not plan/Andre's party

   _____

4. Toshio and Ana/sit/at home/not dine/in a French restaurant

   _____

5. Robin/exercise/at home/not jog/in the park

   _____

6. Mark/walk/his dog/not make/dinner

   _____

A. Build six *Yes/No* questions. Use one word or phrase from each column. Punctuate your sentences correctly.

Was she studying at 5:00 P.M.?

	Sara and Victor	raining	at 5:00 P.M.
was	she	studying	yesterday
were	it	barking	this morning
	the dogs	practicing	

B. Work with a partner. Write six *Yes/No* questions of your own. Then take turns asking and answering them.

A: Were you watching TV at 10:00 P.M. yesterday?
B: Yes, I was.

Complete the conversation about a frightening experience. Use the words in parentheses and the past continuous.

Yuji: Where __were you going__ (you/go)?
　　　　　　　　　　₁

Karen: I was going to Los Angeles.

Yuji: Who _____ (travel) with you?
　　　　　　　　　　　₂

Karen: My brother was.

Yuji: Where _____ (you/sit)?
　　　　　　　　　　　₃

Karen: In the middle section of the plane.

Yuji: What _____ (you/do)
　　　　　　　　　　₄

when you saw the smoke from the engine?

Karen: I was looking out the window.

Yuji: What about the other passengers? How _____ (they/act)?
　　　　　　　　　　　　　　　　　　　　　　　₅

Karen: They were looking around and getting very nervous.

Yuji: And the flight attendants? What _____ (they/do)?
　　　　　　　　　　　　　　　　　　　　₆

Karen: They were helping everyone with their life vests. In the end, we didn't need

them. The pilot landed the plane safely.

C The Past Continuous

Examining Meaning and Use

Read the sentences and answer the questions below. Then discuss your answers and read the Meaning and Use Notes to check them.

   a. At 6:00 yesterday morning it was raining.
   b. At 7:00 I was making breakfast, and the children were getting ready.
   c. Suddenly, I heard a loud crash.

1. Which sentences talk about activities that were in progress at a specific time in the past? What is the form of the verb?

2. Which sentence talks about an event that happened at a specific time but did not continue? What is the form of the verb?

Meaning and Use Notes

Activities in Progress at a Specific Past Time

1A Use the past continuous to talk about activities that were in progress at a specific time in the past. The activities began before the specific time and might also have continued after that time.

A: What **were** you **doing** at 8:00 P.M.?   A: Why was the teacher angry yesterday?
B: I **was watching** TV.   B: Because the students **were talking**.

1B The simple past and the past continuous are different. Use the past continuous for activities in progress at a specific time. Use the simple past for actions that happened at a specific time but did not continue

Activity in Progress   *Actions That Happened but Did Not Continue*
At 5:00 P.M. Marta **was reading**.   Suddenly, the phone **rang**. She **answered** it.

Simultaneous Activities

2A Use the past continuous to talk about two or more activities that were in progress at the same time.

We **were telling** jokes and **laughing**.
I **was sleeping**, and Linda **was taking** a shower.

2B We often use *while* instead of *and* to connect two activities that were happening at the same time.

I was washing the dishes **while** Eva was baking a cake.

While Eva was baking a cake, I was washing the dishes.

Stative Verbs

3 We do not usually use stative verbs in the past continuous. We use the simple past instead.

I **knew** all their names.

*I was knowing all their names (INCORRECT)

C1 **Listening for Meaning and Use** ► Notes 1A, 1B

Listen to each sentence. Is it about an activity that was in progress or about an action that was not in progress? Check (✓) the correct column.

	ACTIVITY IN PROGRESS	ACTION NOT IN PROGRESS
1.	✓	
2.		
3.		
4.		
5.		
6.		
7.		
8.		

Complete this description of a historic disaster that occurred in Lakehurst, New Jersey, in 1937. Use the verbs in parentheses. Think about each verb. Use the past continuous for activities in progress, or the simple past for actions that happened but did not continue.

The *Hindenburg* was a large balloon airship. It _____made_____ (make)
1

its last trip on May 6, 1937. On that day it _____ (rain), and the
2

wind _____ (blow) hard. At exactly 7:00 P.M. the *Hindenburg*
3

_____ (begin) to descend. A few seconds later, a fire
4

_____ (start) aboard the airship. At that moment, many photographers
5

_____ (take) pictures, and a reporter _____ (describe) the
6   7

event. However, at first no one _____ (notice) anything strange. Then
8

suddenly, everyone on the ground _____ (see) smoke. The *Hindenburg*
9

_____ (burn)! Just 37 seconds later, the balloon _____ (fall)
10   11

from the sky, and _____ (hit) the ground. Miraculously, 62 of the 97
12

people on board _____ (survive) the disaster.
13

The *Hindenburg*

A. Read these opening paragraphs of two stories. Circle the verbs that show activities in progress at a specific time.

On that June day I (was walking) in the park. It was a beautiful day. It was warm and bright. The sun was shining, and the birds were singing. I was walking near the lake. Suddenly, I heard a woman's voice. She was singing softly in a strange language. I followed the sound of her voice.

One night I was at home with my brother Danny. The weather was terrible. It (was snowing,) and the wind was blowing. We were watching a scary movie on TV. In the movie, a monster was chasing two young boys. The boys were running away from the monster, and they were screaming. Suddenly, we heard a loud crash in the kitchen. We ran to the window and looked out.

B. Continue this story. Write three or four more sentences after the first sentence to describe activities in progress. Use the past continuous.

Last week I had a very strange experience. I was walking to work . . .

_____

_____

_____

Suddenly, I saw a bright light in the sky.

In a fire drill, people practice what to do in case of a real fire. This university had a fire drill yesterday. Look at the pictures and complete the sentences about what these people were doing when the fire alarm rang.

1. Pete and Rick _were eating lunch._

4. Yuki _____

2. Tyrone and Jorge _____

5. Steve and Celia _____

3. Mr. Simms _____

6. The students _____

Combining Form, Meaning, and Use

D1 Thinking About Meaning and Use

Complete each conversation. Then discuss your answers in small groups.

1. **A:** You got home at 11:00 last night.

   B: Yes. I _____
   - **a.** visited a friend.
   - **(b.)** was visiting a friend.
   - **c.** visiting a friend.

2. **A:** Was the weather bad this morning?

   B: _____
   - **a.** No. The sun was shining.
   - **b.** Yes. The sun shone.
   - **c.** Yes. It's raining.

3. **A:** Hi Mike. Did I wake you up?

   B: _____
   - **a.** No, I slept.
   - **b.** No, I am sleeping.
   - **c.** No, I wasn't sleeping.

4. **A:** Did Gloria come home late?

   B: I don't think so. She _____ in her room at 9:00 last night.
   - **a.** studied
   - **b.** was studying
   - **c.** studying

5. **A:** Why was John angry last night?

   B: _____
   - **a.** He was trying to study while Dan was playing loud music.
   - **b.** Dan is playing loud music.
   - **c.** No. Dan wasn't playing loud music.

6. **A:** Did you own a bike ten years ago?

   B: Yes. I _____ a red mountain bike.
   - **a.** owning
   - **b.** owned
   - **c.** own

7. **A:** Your phone line was busy a moment ago.

   B: Yes. I _____ to Nedra.
   - **a.** am talking
   - **b.** was talking
   - **c.** talk

8. **A:** Did you sleep well?

   B: No. The children _____ a lot of noise.
   - **a.** were making
   - **b.** make
   - **c.** making

Some of these sentences have errors. Find the errors and correct them.

1. We were ~~work~~ *working* at 10:00 A.M.

2. Where was she going?

3. He wasn't wanting any food.

4. We looked up and they are coming.

5. We were working hard while the children watching TV.

6. I didn't go because I was having a bad cold.

▶ Beyond the Classroom

Searching for Authentic Examples

Look for examples of the past continuous in news stories in English-language newspapers and magazines, or on the Internet. Find three examples. Write them in your notebook. Share your examples with the class.

Speaking

Follow the steps below to prepare a one-minute presentation for your classmates.

1. Think of a disaster or news event during your lifetime. Use these questions to make notes.

   • When did it happen?
   • What were you doing at the time?
   • How did you hear about it?
   • How did you feel?

2. Use your answers to prepare your presentation for your classmates. Remember to use the past continuous to describe past events in progress. Use the simple past to describe events that were not in progress.

Last year my best friend was coming to my house for her winter vacation. She was traveling by train from Washington, D.C., to New York. I was cleaning the house and listening to the radio. Suddenly, I heard a news announcement about a train crash outside of Washington. Was it my friend's train? I called her cell phone. My hands were shaking. Luckily, she was safe. It wasn't her train. . . .

Appendices

1 Spelling of Regular and Irregular Plural Nouns

Regular Plural Nouns

1. For most plural nouns, add *-s* to the base form.

apple — apples	lake — lakes
flower — flowers	river — rivers

2. If the base form ends with the letter *s, z, sh, ch,* or *x,* add *-es.*

box — boxes	fax — faxes
bush — bushes	gas — gases

3. If the base form ends with a consonant + *y*, change *y* to *i* and add *-es*.
   (Compare vowel + *y*: boy — boys; toy — toys.)

   baby — babies
   balcony — balconies
   dictionary — dictionaries

4. If the base form ends with a consonant + *o*, add *-s* or *-es*. Some words take *-s*,
   some words take *-es*, some take both *-s* and *-es*. (Compare vowel + *o*: radio —
   radios; zoo — zoos.)

-s	**-es**	**Both -s and -es**
auto — autos	potato — potatoes	tornado — tornados/tornadoes
photo — photos	tomato — tomatoes	volcano — volcanos/volcanoes
piano — pianos		zero — zeros/zeroes
radio — radios		

5. If the base form of certain nouns ends with a single *f* or in *fe*, change the *f* or *fe* to
   v and add *-es*.

   calf — calves
   shelf — shelves
   knife — knives

Exceptions

belief — beliefs
chief — chiefs
roof — roofs
scarf — scarfs/scarves

Irregular Plural Nouns

Singular – Plural

child – children	goose – geese	person – people
fish – fish	man – men	tooth – teeth
foot – feet	mouse – mice	woman – women

② Common Noncount Nouns

Solids
bread
butter
chalk
cheese
chocolate
fish
meat
pasta
rope
soap

Gases
air
carbon dioxide
oxygen
smoke
steam

Materials
cotton
glass
gold
iron
metal
plastic
silver
steel
wood
wool

Liquids
coffee
cream
gasoline
juice
milk
oil
rain
shampoo
soda
soup
tea
toothpaste
water

Grains and Powders
cereal
detergent
dust
flour
pepper
rice
salt
sand
sugar
wheat

Feelings and Ideas
fear
freedom
happiness
independence
information
knowledge
love
sadness
time
work

School Subjects
biology
economics
English
history
mathematics
physical education
physics
science

Activities
baseball
basketball
chess
football
hiking
reading
soccer
swimming
tennis

General Categories
candy
clothing
education
equipment
food
fruit
furniture
jewelry
luggage
money
weather
work

❸ Spelling of Verbs Ending in *-ing*

1. For most verbs, add *-ing* to the base form of the verb.

   sleep — sleeping   talk — talking

2. If the base form ends in a single *e*, drop the *e* and add *-ing* (exception: be – being).

   live — living   write — writing

3. If the base form ends in *ie*, change *ie* to *y* and add *-ing*.

   die — dying   lie — lying

4. If the base form of a one-syllable verb ends with a single vowel + consonant, double the final consonant and add *-ing*. (Compare two vowels + consonant: eat — eating.)

   hit — hitting   stop — stopping

5. If the base form of a verb with two or more syllables ends in a single vowel + consonant, double the final consonant only if the stress is on the final syllable. Do not double the final consonant if the stress is not on the final syllable.

   admit — admitting   begin — beginning   develop — developing   listen — listening

6. Do not double the final consonants *x*, *w*, and *y*.

   fix — fixing   grow — growing   obey — obeying

❹ Spelling of Verbs Ending in *–s* and *–es*

1. For most third-person singular verbs, add *–s* to the base form.

   live – lives
   swim – swims

2. If the base form ends with the letter *s*, *z*, *sh*, *ch*, or *x*, add *–es*.

   miss – misses
   teach—teaches

3. If the base form ends with a consonant + *y*, change *y* to *i* and add *–es*.

   study – studies
   try – tries

4. If the base form ends with a consonant + *o*, *–es*.

   do – does
   go – goes

5 Pronunciation of Verbs and Nouns Ending in -s and -es

1. If the base form of the verb or noun ends with the sound /s/, /z/, /ʃ/, /ʒ/, /tʃ/, /dʒ/, or /ks/, then pronounce -es as an extra syllable /ɪz/.

Verbs		Nouns	
slice — slices	watch — watches	price — prices	inch — inches
lose — loses	judge — judges	size — sizes	language — languages
wash — washes	relax — relaxes	dish — dishes	tax — taxes

2. If the base form ends with the voiceless sound /p/, /t/, /k/, /f/, or /θ/, then pronounce -s and -es as /s/.

Verbs		Nouns	
sleep — sleeps	work — works	grape — grapes	book — books
hit — hits	laugh — laughs	cat — cats	cuff — cuffs

3. If the base form ends with any other consonant or with a vowel sound, then pronounce -s and -es as /z/.

Verbs	Nouns
learn — learns	name — names
go — goes	boy — boys

6 Spelling of Verbs Ending in -ed

1. To form the simple past of most regular verbs, add -ed to the base form.

brush — brushed   play — played

2. If the base form ends with e, just add -d.

close — closed   live — lived

3. If the base form ends with a consonant + y, change the y to i and add -ed. (Compare vowel +y: play — played; enjoy — enjoyed.)

study — studied   dry — dried

4. If the base form of a one-syllable verb ends with a single vowel + consonant, double the final consonant and add -ed.

plan — planned   shop — shopped

5. If the base form of a verb with two or more syllables ends with a single vowel + consonant, double the final consonant and add -ed only when the stress is on the final syllable. Do not double the final consonant if the stress is not on the final syllable.

prefér — preferred   énter — entered

6. Do not double the final consonants x, w, and y.

fix — fixed   snow — snowed   stay — stayed

7 Pronunciation of Verbs Ending in *-ed*

1. If the base form of the verb ends with the sounds /t/ or /d/, then pronounce *-ed* as an extra syllable /ɪd/.

/t/	/d/
start — started	need — needed
wait — waited	decide — decided

2. If the base form ends with the voiceless sounds /p/, /k/, /f/, /s/, /ʃ/, /tʃ/, or /ks/, then pronounce *-ed* as /t/.

jump — jumped	laugh — laughed	wish — wished	fax — faxed
look — looked	slice — sliced	watch — watched	

3. If the base form ends with the voiced sounds /b/, /g/, /dʒ/, /m/, /n/, /ŋ/, /l/, /r/, /ð/, /v/, /z/, or with a vowel, then pronounce *-ed* as /d/.

rob — robbed	hum — hummed	call — called	wave — waved
brag — bragged	rain — rained	order — ordered	close — closed
judge — judged	bang — banged	bathe — bathed	play — played

8 Irregular Verbs

Base Form	Simple Past	Base Form	Simple Past	Base Form	Simple Past
be	was/were	dive	dove (OR dived)	go	went
become	became	do	did	grow	grew
begin	began	draw	drew	hang	hung
bend	bent	drink	drank	have	had
bite	bit	drive	drove	hear	heard
blow	blew	eat	ate	hide	hid
break	broke	fall	fell	hit	hit
bring	brought	feed	fed	hold	held
build	built	feel	felt	hurt	hurt
buy	bought	fight	fought	keep	kept
catch	caught	find	found	know	knew
choose	chose	fly	flew	lay (= put)	laid
come	came	forget	forgot	lead	led
cost	cost	freeze	froze	leave	left
cut	cut	get	got	lend	lent
dig	dug	give	gave	let	let

Base Form	Simple Past	Base Form	Simple Past	Base Form	Simple Past
lose	lost	sell	sold	take	took
make	made	send	sent	teach	taught
meet	met	shoot	shot	tear	tore
pay	paid	show	showed	tell	told
put	put	shut	shut	think	thought
quit	quit	sing	sang	throw	threw
read	read	sit	sat	understand	understood
ride	rode	sleep	slept	wake	woke
ring	rang	speak	spoke	wear	wore
run	ran	spend	spent	win	won
say	said	steal	stole	write	wrote
see	saw	swim	swam		

9 Common Adjectives

Quality/Opinion	Size	Color	Age	Origin	Shape
athletic	big	black	ancient	African	oval
awful	huge	blue	antique	American	rectangular
bright	large	brown	modern	Asian	round
brilliant	little	green	new	Australian	square
cheap	long	grey	old	Brazilian	triangular
cloudy	narrow	orange	old-fashioned	Canadian	
delicious	small	pink	young	Chinese	
expensive	short	purple		European	
famous	tall	red		French	
fantastic	thick	white		German	
handsome	thin	yellow		Indian	
intelligent	tiny			Italian	
interesting	wide			Japanese	
noisy				Korean	
rainy				Latin American	
serious				Middle Eastern	
strong				South American	
terrible				Spanish	
unusual					
useless					
valuable					
wonderful					

10 Adjectives with Two Comparative and Superlative Forms

Adjective	Comparative	Superlative
friendly	friendlier	the friendliest
	more friendly	the most friendly
handsome	handsomer	the handsomest
	more handsome	the most handsome
happy	happier	the happiest
	more happy	the most happy
polite	politer	the politest
	more polite	the most polite
quiet	quieter	the quietest
	more quiet	the most quiet

11 Contractions with Verb and Modal Forms

Contractions with *Be*

I am = I'm
you are = you're
he is = he's
she is = she's
it is = it's
we are = we're
you are = you're
they are = they're

I am not = I'm not
you are not = you're not / you aren't
he is not = he's not / he isn't
she is not = she's not / she isn't
it is not = it's not / it isn't
we are not = we're not / we aren't
you are not = you're not / you aren't
they are not = they're not / they aren't

Contractions with *Will*

I will = I'll
you will = you'll
he will = he'll
she will = she'll
it will = it'll
we will = we'll
you will = you'll
they will = they'll

will not = won't

Contractions with *Was* and *Were*

was not = wasn't
were not = weren't

Contractions with *Be Going To*

I am going to	=	I'm going to
you are going to	=	you're going to
he is going to	=	he's going to
she is going to	=	she's going to
it is going to	=	it's going to
we are going to	=	we're going to
you are going to	=	you're going to
they are going to	=	they're going to
you are not going to	=	you're not going to / you aren't going to

Contractions with *Do* and *Did*

do not	=	don't
does not	=	doesn't
did not	=	didn't

Contractions with *Can,*
Could and *Should*

cannot	=	can't
could not	=	couldn't
should not	=	shouldn't

12 Answers to Exercises

C3: page 179

		PLACE OF BIRTH	YEAR OF BIRTH
2.	Columbus	Italy	1451 A.D.
3.	Confucius	China	about 551 B.C.
4.	Marie Curie	Poland	1867 A.D.
5.	Einstein	Germany	1879 A.D.
6.	Picasso	Spain	1881 A.D.
7.	Rembrandt	the Netherlands	1606 A.D.
8.	Shakespeare	England	1564 A.D.

13 Phonetic Symbols

Vowels

i	see /si/	u	too /tu/	oʊ	go /goʊ/
ɪ	sit /sɪt/	ʌ	cup /kʌp/	ər	bird /bərd/
ɛ	ten /tɛn/	ə	about /əˈbaʊt/	ɪr	near /nɪr/
æ	cat /kæt/	eɪ	say /seɪ/	ɛr	hair /hɛr/
ɑ	hot /hɑt/	aɪ	five /faɪv/	ɑr	car /kɑr/
ɔ	saw /sɔ/	ɔɪ	boy /bɔɪ/	ɔr	north /nɔrθ/
ʊ	put /pʊt/	aʊ	now /naʊ/	ʊr	tour /tʊr/

Consonants

p	pen /pɛn/	f	fall /fɔl/	m	man /mæn/
b	bad /bæd/	v	voice /vɔɪs/	n	no /noʊ/
t	tea /ti/	θ	thin /θɪn/	ŋ	sing /sɪŋ/
t̬	butter /ˈbʌt̬ər/	ð	then /ðɛn/	l	leg /lɛg/
d	did /dɪd/	s	so /soʊ/	r	red /rɛd/
k	cat /kæt/	z	zoo /zu/	y	yes /yɛs/
g	got /gɑt/	ʃ	she /ʃi/	w	wet /wɛt/
tʃ	chin /tʃɪn/	ʒ	vision /ˈvɪʒn/	x	Chanukah /ˈxɑnəkə/
dʒ	June /dʒun/	h	how /haʊ/		

Glossary of Grammar Terms

ability modal *See* **modal of ability**.

action Something that you do, usually involving movement, such as *open a door, drink some water, wash your face.*

action verb A verb that describes a thing that someone or something does. An action verb does not describe a state or condition.

> Sam **rang** the bell.
> I **eat** soup for lunch.
> It **rains** a lot here.

activity A lot of action or movement over a period of time, such as *running, dancing, eating, swimming.*

adjective A word that describes or modifies the meaning of a noun.

> the **orange** car
> a **strange** noise

adverb A word that describes or modifies the meaning of a verb, another adverb, an adjective, or a sentence. Many adverbs answer such questions as *How? When? Where?* or *How often?* They often end in **-ly**.

> She ran **quickly.**   She ran **very** quickly.
> a **really** hot day   **Maybe** she'll leave.

adverb of degree An adverb that makes adjectives or other adverbs stronger or weaker.

> She is **extremely** busy this week.
> He performed **very** well during the exam.
> He was **somewhat** surprised by her response.

adverb of frequency An adverb that tells how often a situation occurs. Adverbs of frequency range in meaning from *all of the time* to *none of the time.*

> She **always** eats breakfast.
> He **never** eats meat.

adverb of manner An adverb that answers the question *How?* and describes the way someone does something or the way something happens. Adverbs of manner usually end in **-ly**.

> He walked **slowly.**
> It rained **heavily** all night.

adverb of opinion An adverb that expresses an opinion about an entire sentence or idea.

> **Luckily,** we missed the traffic.
> We couldn't find a seat on the train, **unfortunately.**

adverb of time An adverb that answers the question *When?* and refers to either a specific time or a more indefinite time.

> Let's leave **tonight** instead of **tomorrow.**
> They **recently** opened a new store.

adverbial phrase A phrase that functions as an adverb.

> Amy spoke **very softly.**

affirmative statement A sentence that does not have a negative verb.

> Linda went to the movies.

agree To have a grammatical relationship with. In English subjects and verbs agree in person and number, for example, *I am . . . , You are . . . , He is . . .*

agreement The subject and verb of a clause must agree in number. If the subject is singular, the verb form is also singular. If the subject is plural, the verb form is also plural.

> **He comes** home early.   **They come** home early.

article The words **a, an,** and **the** in English. Articles are used to introduce and identify nouns.

> **a** potato   **an** onion   **the** supermarket

auxiliary verb A verb that is used before main verbs (or other auxiliary verbs) in a sentence. Auxiliary verbs are usually used in questions and negative sentences. **Do, have,** and **be** can act as auxiliary verbs. Modals (**may, can, will,** and so on) are also auxiliary verbs.

Do you have the time?

I **have** never been to Italy.

The car **was** speeding.

I **may** be late.

base form The form of a verb without any verb endings; the infinitive form without *to*. Also called *simple form*.

sleep   be   stop

clause A group of words that has a subject and a verb. *See also* **dependent clause** and **main clause**.

If I leave, . . .

The rain stopped.

. . . when he speaks.

. . . that I saw.

common noun A noun that refers to any of a class of people, animals, places, things, or ideas. Common nouns are not capitalized.

man   cat   city   pencil   grammar

comparative A form of an adjective, adverb, or noun that is used to express differences between two items or situations.

This book is **heavier than** that one.

He runs **more quickly than** his brother.

A CD costs **more money than** a cassette.

consonant A speech sound that is made by partly or completely stopping the air as it comes out of the mouth. For example, with the sounds /p/, /d/, and /g/, the air is completely stopped. With the sounds /s/, /f/, and /l/, the air is partly stopped.

contraction The combination of two words into one by omitting certain letters and replacing them with an apostrophe.

I will = **I'll**   we are = **we're**   are not = **aren't**

count noun A common noun that you can count as an individual thing. It usually has both a singular and a plural form.

orange — oranges   woman — women

definite article The word **the** in English. It is used to identify nouns based on information the speaker and listener share about the noun. The definite article is also used for making general statements about a whole class or group of nouns.

Please give me **the** key.

The scorpion is dangerous.

demonstrative adjective **This, that, these,** and **those** are demonstrative adjectives when they occur before nouns. They tell whether the noun is near or far from the speaker.

This house is nice. **That** house isn't.

These books are due at the library. **Those** books aren't.

demonstrative pronoun **This, that, these,** and **those** are demonstrative pronouns when they take the place of a demonstrative adjective + noun.

This is new. (This book is new.)

That is old. (That book is old.)

These are ready. (These cookies are ready.)

Those aren't ready. (Those cookies aren't ready.)

dependent clause A clause that cannot stand alone as a sentence because it depends on the main clause to complete the meaning of the sentence. Also called *subordinate clause*.

I'm going home **after he calls.**

determiner A word such as **a, an, the, this, that, these, those, my, some, a few,** and **three** that is used before a noun to limit its meaning in some way.

those videos

direct object A noun or pronoun that refers to a person or thing that is directly affected by the action of a verb.

John wrote **a letter.**

Please buy **some milk.**

first person One of the three classes of personal pronouns. First person refers to the person *(I)* or people *(we)* who are actually speaking or writing.

formal A style of speech or writing where the speaker or writer is very careful about pronunciation, choice of words, and sentence structure. Formal language is used at official functions, ceremonies, speeches, in the law and in other types of serious writing.

> "Ladies and Gentlemen, allow me to introduce a man to whom I owe a great deal of gratitude . . . "

future A time that is to come. The future is expressed in English with **will, be going to,** the simple present, or the present continuous. These different forms of the future often have different meanings and uses.

> I **will** help you later.
> David **is going to** call later.
> The train **leaves** at 6:05 this evening.
> I**'m driving** to Toronto tomorrow.

general quantity expression A quantity expression that indicates whether a quantity or an amount is large or small. It does not give an exact amount.

> **a lot of** cookies   **a little** flour
> **a few** people   **some** milk

general statement A generalization about a whole class or group of nouns.

> Whales are mammals.
> A daffodil is a flower that grows from a bulb.

gerund An **-ing** form of a verb that is used in place of a noun or pronoun to name an activity or a state.

> **Skiing** is fun.   He doesn't like **being sick**.

imperative A type of sentence, usually without a subject, that tells someone to do something. The verb is in the base form.

> **Open** your books to page 36.
> **Be** ready at eight.

impersonal *you* The use of the pronoun **you** to refer to people in general rather than a particular person or group of people.

> Nowadays **you** can buy anything on the Internet.

indefinite article The words **a** and **an** in English. Indefinite articles introduce a noun as a member of a class of nouns or make generalizations about a whole class or group of nouns.

> Please hand me **a** pencil.
> **An** ocean is **a** large body of water.

independent clause *See* **main clause**.

indirect object A noun or pronoun used after some verbs that refers to the person who receives the direct object of a sentence.

> John wrote a letter **to Mary**.
> Please buy some milk **for us**.

infinitive A verb form that includes **to** + the base form of a verb. An infinitive is used in place of a noun or pronoun to name an activity or state expressed by a verb.

> Do you like **to swim**?

informal A style of speech, and sometimes writing, used in everyday conversations between friends, co-workers, and family members. In informal speech, the speaker is casual about pronunciation, choice of words, and sentence structure. Informal speech is often fast speech with a lot of reduced and contracted forms. Short notes, e-mail messages, and written dialogues are often informal.

information question A question that begins with a **wh-** word.

> Where does she live?
> Who lives here?

intonation The change in pitch, loudness, syllable length, and rhythm in spoken language.

intransitive verb A verb that cannot be followed by an object.

> We finally **arrived**.

irregular verb A verb that does not form the simple past by adding *-d* or *-ed* endings.

> put — put
> buy — bought

main clause A clause that can be used by itself as a sentence. Also called *independent clause*.

> I'm going home.

main verb A verb that can be used alone in a sentence. A main verb can also occur with an auxiliary verb.

> I **ate** lunch at 11:30.
> Kate can't **eat** lunch today.

modal The auxiliary verbs **can, could, may, might, must, should, will,** and **would.** They modify the meaning of a main verb by expressing ability, authority, formality, politeness, or various degrees of certainty. Also called *modal auxiliary.*

You **should** take something for your headache.

Applicants **must** have a high school diploma.

modal of ability **Can** and **could** are called modals of ability when they express the ability to do something.

He **can** speak Arabic and English.

Can you play the piano?

Yesterday we **couldn't** leave during the storm.

Seat belts **can** save lives.

modal of permission **May, could,** and **can** are called modals of permission when they are used to ask for, give, or refuse permission to do something.

A: **May** I leave early?

B: Yes, you **can.**

A: Mom, **could** I stay up late tonight?

B: No, you **may not.** You have school tomorrow.

modal auxiliary *See* **modal.**

modify To add to or change the meaning of a word.

Adjectives modify nouns (**expensive** cars).

Adverbs modify verbs (**very** fast).

negative statement A sentence with a negative verb.

I **didn't see** that movie.

He **isn't** happy.

non-action verb *See* **stative verb**

noncount noun A common noun that cannot be counted. A noncount noun has no plural form and cannot occur with **a, an,** or a number.

information   mathematics   weather

noun A word that typically refers to a person, animal, place, thing, or idea.

Tom   rabbit   store   computer   mathematics

noun phrase A phrase formed by a noun and its modifiers. A noun phrase can substitute for a noun in a sentence.

She drank **milk.**

She drank **chocolate milk.**

She drank **the milk.**

object A noun, pronoun, or noun phrase that follows a transitive verb or a preposition.

He likes **pizza.**

She likes **him.**

Go with **her.**

Steve threw **the ball.**

object pronoun The pronouns **me, you** (sg., pl.), **him, her, it, us,** and **them** are object pronouns when they act as the object of a verb or preposition.

past continuous A verb form that expresses an activity in progress at a specific time in the past. The past continuous is formed with **was** or **were** + verb + **-ing.** Also called *past progressive.*

A: What **were** you **doing** last night
  at eight o'clock?

B: I **was studying.**

past progressive *See* **past continuous.**

phrasal modal A verb that is not a true modal, but has the same meaning as a modal verb. Examples of phrasal modals are **ought to, have to,** and **have got to.**

phrase A group of words that can form a grammatical unit. A phrase can take the form of a noun phrase, verb phrase, adjective phrase, adverbial phrase, or prepositional phrase. This means it can act as a noun, verb, adjective, adverb, or preposition.

The **tall man** left.

Lee **hit the ball.**

The child was **very quiet.**

She spoke **too fast.**

They ran **down the stairs.**

plural The form of a word that refers to more than one person or thing. For example, **cats** and **children** are the plural forms of **cat** and **child.**

preposition A word such as **at, in, on,** or **to,** that links nouns, pronouns, and gerunds to other words.

prepositional phrase A phrase that consists of a preposition followed by a noun or noun phrase.

on Sunday

under the table

present continuous A verb form that indicates that an activity is in progress, temporary, or changing. It is formed with **be** + verb + **-ing**. Also called *present progressive*.

> I**'m watering** the garden.
> Ruth **is working** for her uncle.
> He**'s getting** better.

present progressive *See* **present continuous**.

pronoun A word that can replace a noun or noun phrase. **I, you, he, she, it, mine,** and **yours** are some examples of pronouns.

proper noun A noun that is the name of a particular person, animal, place, thing, or idea. Proper nouns begin with capital letters and are usually not preceded by **the**.

> Peter   Rover   India   Apollo 13   Buddhism

quantity expression A word or words that occur before a noun to express a quantity or amount of that noun.

> **a lot of** rain
> **few** books
> **four** trucks

reduced form A shortened form of a word or phrase that is common in fast, informal speech.

> "Need any help?" (Do you need any help?)
> "I'm gonna call you." (I'm going to call you.)

regular verb A verb that forms the simple past by adding -**ed**, -**d**, or changing **y** to **i** and then adding -**ed** to the simple form.

> hunt — hunted
> love — loved
> cry — cried

response An answer to a question, or a reply to other types of spoken or written language.

> A: Are you hungry?
> B: **Yes, in fact I am. Let's eat.**

second person One of the three classes of personal pronouns. Second person refers to the person (**you,** singular) or people (**you,** plural) who are the listeners or readers.

short answer An answer to a *Yes/No* question that has *yes* or *no* plus the subject and an auxiliary verb.

> A: Do you speak Chinese?
> B: **Yes, I do. / No, I don't.**

simple form *See* **base form**.

simple past A verb tense that expresses actions and situations that were completed at a definite time in the past.

> Carol **ate** lunch.
> She **was** hungry.

simple present A verb tense that expresses general statements, especially about habitual or repeated activities and permanent situations.

> Every morning I **catch** the 8:00 bus.
> The earth **is** round.

singular The form of a word that refers to only one person or thing. For example, **cat** and **child** are the singular forms of **cats** and **children**.

standard form A form of language that is based on the speech and writing of educated native speakers of a language. Standard language is used in the news media and other public speech, in literature, in textbooks, and other academic materials. It is described in dictionaries and grammar books.

state Physical conditions, senses, possession, knowledge, feelings, and measurements are states that are expressed with *be* and other non-action (stative) verbs.

> She **is tall.**
> The flower **smells good.**
> He **owns a house.**

stative verb A type of verb that is not usually used in the continuous form because it expresses a condition or state that is not changing. **Know, love, resemble, see,** and **smell** are some examples. Also called *non-action verb*.

stress The pronunciation of a syllable or word with more force than the pronunciation of surrounding syllables or words. Stressed syllables or words often sound louder and longer than surrounding syllables or words.

> I didn't see **Sara,** I saw **John.**

subject A noun, pronoun, or noun phrase that precedes the verb phrase in a sentence. The subject of a sentence with *be* tells who or what the sentence is about. The subject of a sentence with an action verb tells who did or caused the action.

The park is huge.
Erica kicked the ball.

subject pronoun The pronouns **I, you** (sg., pl.), **he, she, it, we,** and **they** are subject pronouns when they act as the subject of a clause.

subordinate clause *See* **dependent clause.**

superlative A form of an adjective, adverb, or noun used to compare a group of three or more people, things, or actions. The superlative shows that one member of the group has more (or less) than all of the others.

This perfume has **the strongest** scent.
He speaks **the fastest** of all.
That machine makes **the most noise** of the three.

syllable A word or part of a word that contains one vowel sound.

Happy has two syllables: **hap-py**
Dictionary has four syllables: **dic-tion-ar-y**

tense The form of a verb that shows past, present, and future time.

He **lives** in New York now.
He **lived** in Washington two years ago.
He**'ll live** in Toronto next year.

third person One of the three classes of personal pronouns. Third person refers to some person (**he, she**), people (**they**), or thing (**it**) other than the speaker/writer or listener/reader.

time expression A phrase that functions as an adverb of time.

She graduated **three years ago.**
I'll see them **the day after tomorrow.**

transitive verb A verb that is followed by an object.

I **read** the book.

verb A word that refers to an action or a state.

Gina **closed** the window.
Tim **loves** classical music.

verb phrase A phrase that has a main verb and any objects, adverbs, or dependent clauses that complete the meaning of the verb in the sentence.

She **is talking.**
Who **called you**?
He **walked slowly.**

voiced Refers to speech sounds that are made by vibrating the vocal cords. Examples of voiced sounds are /b/, /d/, and /g/.

bat   **d**ot   **g**et

voiceless Refers to speech sounds that are made without vibrating the vocal cords. Examples of voiceless sounds are /p/, /t/, and /f/.

u**p**   i**t**   i**f**

vowel A speech sound that is made with the lips and teeth open. The air from the lungs is not blocked at all. For example, the sounds /a/, /o/, and /i/ are vowels.

wh- **word** Who, whom, what, where, when, why, how, and which are **wh-** words. They are used to ask questions and to connect clauses.

Yes/No **question** A question that can be answered with the words **yes** or **no.**

Can you drive a car?
Does he live here?

Index

This Index is for the full and split editions. Entries for Volume A are in bold.